VACCINE RHETORICS

VACCINE RHETORICS

Heidi Yoston
Lawrence

THE OHIO STATE UNIVERSITY PRESS

COLUMBUS

Library of Congress Cataloging-in-Publication Data is available online at catalog.loc.gov.

Cover design by Christian Fuenfhausen
Text design by Juliet Williams
Type set in Adobe Minion Pro

♾ The paper used in this publication meets the minimum requirements of the American National Standard for Information Sciences—Permanence of Paper for Printed Library Materials. ANSI Z39.48-1992.

CONTENTS

TABLES

A Starting Point

I BEGAN researching vaccination controversy in 2010 while supporting what would later become the Vaccination Research Group at Virginia Tech. Frankly, I started off relatively agnostic on the issue. I had never gotten a flu vaccine but was otherwise fully vaccinated and didn't have children to vaccinate. I knew that some people refused vaccines, but I honestly didn't see what the big deal was. Nevertheless, as a dutiful researcher, I dove in, eager to see what it was all about.

I was quickly hooked. Intrigued by the problem, its many passionate and colorful actors, and seemingly intractable path to resolution, I found new questions and opportunities for rhetorical intervention at every turn the research took. Over the years to follow, I completed dozens of presentations, qualitative interview studies, and survey studies and read hundreds of articles about vaccination and its attendant controversies as I completed a dissertation and subsequent publications on the topic.

And then I got pregnant and had a baby boy.

Going into motherhood, I knew that I would vaccinate my child, but I was always deeply ambivalent about rotavirus vaccine,[1] which protects against rotavirus infection. Rotavirus is a serious disease. At its best, it is essentially very bad diarrhea. At its worst, it can cause severe dehydration and malnutri-

---

1. Two vaccines were available against rotavirus during the timeframe under discussion here, Rotarix and Rotateq. I do not know which actual brand my son's pediatrics office administered.

tion, and even lead to death. So I could see the benefits and necessity of the vaccine. Yet I mostly perceived my son to be at low risk for contracting or spreading it, and I felt confident that my access to resources would make it manageable even if he did somehow get it. It also isn't a required vaccine for school entry in my state, so I knew that by skipping it, my son wouldn't have to "catch up" on the vaccine later. So the risks of the vaccine side effects—a cranky baby, maybe some diarrhea, even the rare chance of intussusception—didn't quite seem worth it. I reflected on my position toward rotavirus and the vaccine in a 2016 article, which I wrote when my son was six weeks old:

> I also planned to refuse rotavirus vaccine entirely. He is breastfed and does not attend daycare or have any interaction with other children, so my reasoning was that his risk of contracting or spreading the disease was low. We also live in a populous area with easy access to a variety of health care facilities. If he did contract it, so my thinking went, any complications like dehydration could be easily and quickly addressed before they became dire.
>
> Then I read Kathleen Hennessy's "How a Bout of Rotavirus Made Me Appreciate Vaccines," and, to my surprise, I felt my position on Rotavirus vaccine slip away. (Lawrence, "Fear" 206)

Hennessy's narrative in the above-mentioned excerpt describes her child's back-to-back rotavirus infections. It is a harrowing tale involving sleepless days and nights, endless bleaching of surfaces, and—most worrisome of all—concerns about feeding and weight gain for a sick baby. In response I wrote:

> I have read versions of her story before, of course—both clinical and personal accounts about the duration of the disease, the perniciousness of its infectiousness, the undeniable ick factor, and the very real possibility of a baby becoming severely dehydrated and dying. But Hennessy's narrative made me experience all of those things anew as I pictured myself in her position: desperately trying to feed a sick baby, tensely watching his every breath, and feverishly bleaching surfaces as sleepless days and weeks go by. And then I felt it: fear. (Lawrence, "Fear" 206)

A few weeks later, I got that vaccine for my son. I felt good about it, like I had made the right decision as a parent.

Not long after, he developed a bout of serious gastrointestinal (GI) problems and intolerances, and I grew hesitant as the next rotavirus booster approached. Rotavirus vaccine is an oral vaccine, and after months and months of trial and error trying to figure out what was causing my baby's GI problems, things had finally returned to normal. By the time his appointment arrived, I had decided that I wasn't getting the next booster. Although I in no way associated his problems with the vaccine, I just didn't want to introduce anything that might jeopardize the progress we had made. I communicated my decision to his practitioner as soon as the topic of vaccines came up. She disagreed, citing research that his GI problems made him even more susceptible to rotavirus, noting how devastating it might be to his progress if he were to become severely ill, and describing how safe and effective the vaccine was. I wasn't persuaded.

After leaving the appointment where I refused the vaccine, I made the following voice note to myself on the drive home:

> Overall, I think that the most difficult part of it was that it was just deeply uncomfortable. [The practitioner] and I were having this very nice appointment. We were communicating really nicely. Everything was really friendly. She was really excited, talking about how cute [my son] was. It was a very nice interaction.
>
> Then, when I said I didn't want to do the rotavirus vaccine, it was like things changed, like the dynamic really shifted.
>
> I felt *discomfort*. I didn't feel irritation. It didn't feel antagonistic. It felt more just like, "Why are you doing this? We were all getting along so well, and now you're not doing what I say, and now this is a point of tension."

feelings of appt. dictated by "Dr. ?"

As it would turn out, this would be the last time I met with that practitioner, since she left the practice soon after. I regretted that this was our last interaction. She meant a lot to me. She had shepherded me through the first few months of new motherhood and been really supportive of breastfeeding. She had helped us through a bad respiratory infection, along with the GI problems. I trusted her and liked her and was thankful for everything she had done. And then this happened, and it just felt like this interaction created a fissure in our relationship, one that I never had the chance to repair.

I share this story for three reasons related to the purpose of this book. First, to articulate my position: I consider myself a vaccinating parent and a provaccine adult. I wholeheartedly support vaccines and vaccine mandates. I know that vaccines are safe and effective and important. I also felt that it was my responsibility to skip a booster that I felt provided uncertain benefit and possible increased risk to my son. All of these things are, to me, logical, internally consistent, and a part of the way I enact what I believe to be good parenting. Yet other stakeholders—parents, practitioners, policymakers alike—might lump me in with "anti-vaxxers," shorthand for someone who is anti-science,

positionality

stupid, a Jenny McCarthy acolyte, and possibly even a negligent parent who deserves a call to Child Protective Services (CPS) because I refused a vaccine for my child. Pushing back against such rigid, unproductive categorizations and understandings of vaccine skepticisms is one purpose of this book.

Second, I also share my story to outline an experience interacting with a medical practitioner about vaccines in a less than positive way as an example of how rhetoric might uniquely help attenuate existing discord. Although I cannot know how my child's practitioner felt about my refusal, I do know how I felt—uncomfortable, anxious, questioned in my ability to make good decisions on behalf of my child, and nervous about what that meant for my standing in the practice. I can also read the signs of her discomfort in the events that followed: she walked out of our appointment, retrieved a waiver form that I had to sign, and then left again without another word to me or my child, leaving the nurse to administer the remaining vaccines that he was receiving that day. Again, I cannot know what was in her head, but she seemed angry and disappointed at not being trusted. It really wasn't about me trusting or not trusting her, though. I didn't trust the vaccine itself. I knew the risks and benefits. I knew every argument for and against the vaccine. I knew that she was absolutely making the best recommendation she could and that no one would be more surprised than she if his GI problems resurfaced after the vaccination. My decision wasn't rooted in a lack of trust in her expertise; it was rooted in my own experiences with a sick child, my own previous history as a patient and new mother, and mostly my distrust of the object itself and its unknown potential for good as well as harm. She couldn't have done anything about any of that. Attempting to decouple the relationship many make between vaccine refusal and a rejection of physicians' expertise or scientific knowledge broadly is a second purpose of this book.

Finally, I share this story to demonstrate how vaccines change over time for all of us as individual patients, for parents, and for citizens in a public who rely on community-level protections to keep us from getting diseases. We might think we support—or don't support—vaccines or vaccine mandates, but then something changes, altering our relationship to our own bodies, our definitions of personal responsibilities, and our resulting views on the prospect of being vaccinated. Vaccination is constantly evolving, emblematic of our experiences in our bodies, in our families, and in our communities. An understanding of vaccination's embodied materiality and how it shapes the democratic, deliberative decisions we make about vaccines as a society, and how scholars in rhetoric in particular can help facilitate such a shift, is thus a third purpose of this book.

Vaccine Rhetorics is reflective of these purposes and the many other experiences and changes I have observed since I began this research in 2010. Vaccination controversy looks different now than it did nearly a decade ago. In 2010 the recent H1N1 crisis had left public health practitioners worried that they wouldn't be able to conduct a mass vaccination campaign against a serious threat if they ever needed to, because widespread controversy would get in the way. Now, recent outbreaks of measles are prompting changes in laws and policies toward expanding vaccine mandates, with significant and vocal public support. Nationally, California had one of the most permissive vaccination laws at the time, which left specific schools vulnerable to contagious vaccine-preventable diseases like pertussis and measles. As of this writing in 2019, however, vaccination rates in California are rising, following the 2015 policy change that removed all exemptions except in the case of medical contraindication. Consequently, a long-standing problem in California is being resolved so rapidly that, in another decade, the entire situation could be resolved. But new problems will take its place as new politicians take up the banner of vaccination (or antivaccination) during their campaigns, new diseases emerge, and new vulnerable populations are identified. In that same decade to come, every one of us will see our own positions on vaccination change as we become parents, get sick and then hopefully well again, enter old age, or change our living situations or occupations. We may also see the shots themselves change as diseases are eradicated or new safety concerns change their formulations. They may no longer be shots at all if new technologies like patch-based, inhaled, or food-based vaccines take favor.

Amid all those changes that may come to pass, one thing is certain: vaccines—and all the concerns, questions, and controversy about them—will still exist. As a multiple, complex thing, vaccines don't *just* gain their power and importance through their life-saving potential or value to public health. Vaccines have status because of their power to mediate modern life, making vaccination an evolving scientific and social experience as well as a deeply embodied and material one all at the same time, meaning that some degree of public scrutiny will always be present.

Vaccine Rhetorics attempts to unravel the key components of these complexities of vaccination to expose and examine them, with a goal of finding points for rhetorical intervention to mitigate discord. The goals of this book are therefore threefold—first, for rhetoricians to gain a new paradigm through which to understand large, public controversies involving science, health, and medicine; second, for medical rhetoricians to see how material shapes medicine and science, particularly medical and scientific systems involving infectious disease and preventative health measures; and third, to offer a mechanism through which rhetoricians can address and impact public problems, in addition to analyzing them.

Although vaccination controversy might seem like a monolithic issue where science battles denialists who are simply ill informed or misguided, this text exposes the ways in which the issue is far more complex than such a characterization indicates. Even the most ardent supporter of vaccination might one day be faced with a new requirement that comes with a new risk that might demand a reconsideration of support. As my own story about rotavirus reveals, these changes occur daily, may be heightened or resolved over time, and ultimately impact and are impacted by our experiences as we traverse medical systems. Understanding and accepting the evolution of the social, cultural, and embodied experience of being vaccinated, this text maintains, is the starting point for a rhetorical approach to vaccination.

ACKNOWLEDGMENTS

THIS BOOK took a bigger village than I ever could have imagined, and I'm humbled by the time, efforts, and support that everyone listed here has graciously extended to me over the years to ensure that this work exists.

The short list of most sincere thanks go to . . .

Everyone who participated in the research in this book. I want to thank the physicians who participated in the research interviews that are the subject of chapter 1, the students whose interviews on flu and flu vaccine are analyzed in chapter 4, and participants in the surveys and pilot studies that informed the methods used here. Without their time commitment and candor, this work—and the knowledge they have helped to create about what people think about vaccines—would not have been possible.

Everyone who made the publication of this book possible. I want to thank my editor at The Ohio State University Press, Tara Cyphers, Kristina Wheeler, and the anonymous reviewers of this manuscript. Your feedback and belief in this work was instrumental in helping me articulate the book's mission, find my voice, and make the claims I needed to make as I revised. I also want to thank Mae Bonem, Kellie Bryan, and Rachael Graham Lussos for their invaluable feedback and editorial assistance, of which I was in dire need.

Colleagues nationally who helped mentor, inform, and advise my work on vaccination. Most sincere thanks go to James Colgrove, Elena Conis, Robert Johnston, and Andrea Kitta for their smart work on vaccination and for taking the time to listen to my ideas and give me feedback and encouragement very early in this research. I also thank leaders in my professional organizations, particularly the Rhetoric Society of America (RSA) and the Association for Teachers of Technical Writing (ATTW), for creating spaces and opportunities for feedback on this work, particularly in the development of the theoretical framing and interview analyses that appear in chapter 1; in this vein, I thank Jeff Bennett, Jenell Johnson, Blake Scott, Cheryl Geisler, and Ellen Barton in particular for providing these spaces and opportunities.

All my colleagues and mentors at Virginia Tech. My eternal thanks go to all of my colleagues, and especially to Brian Gogan, Dan Lawson, Tim Lockridge, Megan O'Neill, Ashley Patriarca, Molly Scanlon, Michelle Seref, and Matt Sharp, for your friendship, laughter, helpful questions, and smarts. I thank Paul Heilker and Carolyn Rude for persuading me to go to Tech in the first place and for guiding me through; Kelly Pender for teaching me so much about rhetoric and how to write about it; Clare Dannenberg and Katy Powell for teaching me career-changing lessons like how to do research, how to think about the world, and how to be a good colleague; and Eva Brumberger, Jim Collier, Jim Dubinsky, Carlos Evia, Diana George, and Kathryn Graham for connecting me to invaluable opportunities at Tech that have shaped me as a writer, a teacher, and a researcher. I also want to thank the members of the Vaccination Research Group at Virginia Tech for their research support, especially Olivia Kasik, Rachael Knight, Karen Spears, and Tarryn Abrahams.

My colleagues at George Mason. I want to thank the entire English department, and Doug Eyman, E. Shelley Reid, and Debra Lattanzi Shutika in particular, for taking a chance on me and providing the time, feedback, and resources necessary to complete this work. I thank Mary Baldwin and Barb Gomperts for making my work happen in key and important ways. I thank Eric Anderson for his long-time counsel and mentorship. I thank my colleagues in Writing and Rhetoric for their support, comradery, and good humor. I also want to thank my colleagues across Mason—Melissa Broeckelman-Post, Susan Lawrence, Emily Ihara, Ellen Serafini, Isidore Dorpenyo, Bonnie Stabile, Ali Weinstein, and Cathy Tompkins in particular—for all the assistance (logistical, emotional, professional, and otherwise) they offered to me at critical moments in this project. A huge thanks to students at GMU for all their research assistance on this and related projects, including PhD students Elizabeth Ferguson, Lourdes Fernandez, Veronica Garrison Joyner, Rachael Graham Lussos, and Norma Smith; MA students Mae Bonem and Luana Shafer; and members of my English 502 class, who assisted with the data collection in chapter 4: Manal Assad, Emily Bourne, Brandon Cantrell,

Paula Ferguson, Lauren Hoerath, Tara McVey, Tamara Moorman, Stephanie Nelson, Kimberlyn Pepe, and Jennifer Stevens.

My closest colleagues and mentors. Amy Reed, thank you for reading my worst drafts and finding the best in them, for your confidence in me when I can't find it for myself, and for being so incredibly smart that your work always makes mine better simply by proximity. Libby Anthony, thank you for letting me laugh, cry, rant, and talk to myself; thank you for navigating some of the scariest and most joyful parts of academe (and life) with me; thank you for everything you taught me about being a good colleague and academic and friend. Byron Hawk, thank you for introducing me to rhetoric, for your invaluable feedback on the introduction to this book, and for the courage you gave me to say what I wanted to say. And of course, to Bernice Hausman. Gratitude and thanks just don't seem like enough—you have inspired and led me to be the scholar, teacher, mentor, and colleague that I am, and I'm forever shaped by everything you have taught me. Thank you so much for all your time and constant, unwavering support.

My friends and family. There is simply not enough space here (or in two or three books) to outline the particulars of your help and how invaluable it has been to me over the years. I want to thank some of my longest-standing mentors and supporters, Steve George, Lettie George, and Steve Lowery, for being such invaluable sources of support to me throughout this work and my career. To my friends Matt Revelle, Jennifer Farrell, Shelley and Mark Rakip, Kellie Bryan, Kimberly Hall, Abby Waldron, Kevin Stoy, Chris Hall, and CJ Waldron; my sisters, Aubree and Hannah Lawrence, and their partners, Austen Hypher and Rob MacCall; and my in-laws, Rodney and Elaine Garner: all I can say is thank you. Thank you for all your tireless support and for making my life as rich as it is. To my parents, Richard and Dorothy Lawrence, thank you for everything you taught me about life and hard work and determination, because I needed every ounce of it to complete this book.

The amazing women who gave their time, labor, and talents to help me write this book by taking care of my son while I worked on it. Specifically, I want to thank (Ms.) Emily Crowley, (Ms.) Diana Wassel, (Ms.) Grace Tompkins, and (Ms.) Liane Chang, in addition to many of the friends and family members listed above.

My husband, Ryan. You—and you alone—made this book and my career happen through the countless ways you have supported me and my efforts during the past twenty years. Of course, you helped with all the usual things— the run for printer paper at the last moment; walking Charlie or feeding Milton and TS, and later Alice and Minerva, when there wasn't a moment to spare; the early-morning and late-night coffee runs; and so on. But, more than that, you kept the Voldemort Project going when I didn't just want to give up on it but insisted that I must give it up, that moving forward was absolutely impossible, and that no good could come of it if I continued. I love you, and I thank you for everything.

And finally, to Nathan. My sweet, beautiful boy. I started writing this book for me and for your dad and the goals we had together, but I finished it for you. I thank you for your patience during the days that this book took my attention away from you and for your insistence during the days that you refused to let this book take my attention away from you. You have taught me balance and love, and I'm so honored to be your mom. I love you so very much, forever and ever.

INTRODUCTION

Retaining Persuasion

IN THE US, school boards, doctors, parents, and citizens have two options when it comes to vaccination: compulsion or persuasion.[1] People are compelled to vaccinate largely through laws and policies that restrict access to essential sites and spaces—namely, schools and jobs—on the basis of vaccination status. As James Colgrove and others have observed, historically compulsion has been highly successful at achieving higher rates of vaccination in the US. Or, as Emily Oster and Geoffrey Kocks most poignantly state: "changing minds on vaccination is very difficult, but it isn't so important when a law can change behavior."

Some could say that in 2019, at the writing of this book, we are in the midst of a robust movement in favor of compulsion in America. The 1905 *Jacobson v. Massachusetts* Supreme Court case set the nationwide precedent allowing states to mandate vaccination, and vaccine mandates for school entry in particular have been imposed to ensure that children are protected from disease.

---

1. This observation is made by a variety of scholars, though I am particularly citing the observations of James Colgrove and Eileen Wang et al., as they have noted the distinctions between compulsory and persuasive tactics in public health responses generally (Colgrove) and compared with other countries without compulsory laws (Wang et al. e82). I also discuss the tensions surrounding this issue of compulsion versus persuasion as a starting point for reconsidering persuasion in the 2018 article "When Patients Question Vaccines: Considering Vaccine Communication through a Material Rhetorical Lens" in the journal *Rhetoric of Health & Medicine*.

Although all states have some law compelling vaccination, all states also have exemptions available for those vaccines, and some states are stricter than others. In 2015 California, previously one of the most permissive states for vaccine exemptions, joined Mississippi and West Virginia as the only three states to allow only medical exemptions to vaccines. In these states, only those with a documented medical contraindication (such as a life-threatening allergy or severe immune suppression that would make vaccination dangerous) can avoid mandatory vaccination. Compulsory tactics abound outside of state-level mandates as well. Increasingly, individual physician offices are adopting stringent policies that require parents and patients to vaccinate or leave their practices, and the American Academy of Pediatrics (AAP) advocated in 2016 for state-level policy changes to remove all nonmedical exemptions across the United States (AAP Committee on Practice and Ambulatory Medicine). Even parenting groups, forums, and media reports encourage parents to ask other parents whether they are vaccinating their children and, if not, prohibit them from participating in those communities (Zibners; Stewart).

What about persuasion, then? Has the issue of vaccination, and its attendant concerns about disease, injury, and personal and community risk, really pressed at the limits of what is possible to persuade people to do? Is it even ethical to leave such important stakes to the messy and imprecise tactics of persuasion? Is compulsion the only answer? Or is there a way to give this issue back some of its rhetoricity?

As a researcher in rhetorical studies, I'm drawn to and invested in the idea that persuasion is still important despite the apparent benefits that compulsion might offer. Persuasion, in its best form, is not coercive but collaborative. Aristotle's definition of rhetoric as "seeing the available means of persuasion" makes rhetoric an analytical, knowledge-making practice that necessitates mutual forms of understanding. Since the Greeks (and before), persuasion has been the hallmark of a democratic public, a discursive act that requires an attention and response to the needs of the public. Resorting to compulsion, in rhetorical terms, is to make situations *arhetorical*: to use sources and structures of power to remove opportunities for persuasion, collaboration, or deliberation. Rather, compulsion forces either compliance or infraction—nondiscursive results that carry real legal, social, and professional consequences.

Beyond my disciplinary investments in rhetoric, the research I have conducted on vaccination controversy indicates the continued need for persuasive, discursive responses to vaccines despite calls for compulsion. Time and time again, vaccination and its related controversies prove to be about more than just rates of uptake for doctors, public health professionals, and parents, pro- and antivaccine alike. For patients (and, most often, parents of patients), one's position on vaccination is not just one decision among many made at the doctor's office, viewed in simple terms of compliance. To vaccinate is to accept risk on behalf of one's community, to accept the risk of an unknown outcome, and often to accept those risks on behalf of babies and children who have no choice or agency of their own yet bear all the consequences. Although the vast majority of medical and health professionals describe themselves as provaccine, the articulation of that support is metered by concerns about fluctuations in the efficacy of flu vaccine, lingering struggles about whether higher vaccination rates are really worth losing patients who need care, or questions about the necessity of the specific schedule outlined by the CDC. In all these cases, vaccination is articulated as a social practice, a way of shaping and crafting one's self in the world as a parent, a patient, a doctor. These individual, embodied, material experiences demonstrate how vaccination is an unstable and uncertain practice that demands deliberation, discussion, and understanding—all the enactments of discourse that persuasion, and thus rhetoric, requires.

Vaccine Rhetorics examines the role that persuasion might play in vaccination controversy in light of calls for compulsion. By applying the theories of rhetoric and the objectives of rhetorical analysis, this text identifies spaces where a rhetorically informed, persuasive approach might open opportunities for discourse and find paths to ameliorate the controversies that have plagued the practice of vaccination for hundreds of years.

ABOUT VACCINATION CONTROVERSY

Before we can craft a rhetorical approach to this controversy, we must address the question: why are vaccines controversial? Vaccination programs have had some of the most far-reaching and expansive impacts on community health and longevity among all public health programs. By the age of five or so, children who follow the CDC's 2018 schedule will receive vaccines to protect against a wide range of diseases: common ailments like rotavirus, devastating diseases like polio, and diseases with extreme complications like Hib. Vaccination continues over the lifespan, with teens and adults routinely getting vaccines to protect against meningococcal meningitis, some strains of human papilloma virus, shingles, various strains of flu, and pneumonia. Moreover, vaccines are safe and effective at reducing cases of disease. Beyond the infamous eradication of smallpox, diseases like diphtheria, polio, and rubella are now nearly unheard of in the US; measles outbreaks are still relatively atypical; and flu vaccines save individuals and communities valuable time, money, and resources by limiting suffering from flu. Why would something so simple, so successful, so undoubtedly beneficial across the lifespan be the subject of discord?

Despite these successes, vaccinations provoke controversy from various components of the public sphere. Since the adoption of the practice in the nineteenth century, vaccinations have been a target of skepticism because they are a unique type of procedure, for three reasons.

First, vaccinations are given to healthy people for the prevention of disease. Therefore, our expectations of safety and efficacy are heightened; risks must be nominal, involving only minor discomfort or side effects, and serious risks must be exceedingly rare. Second, vaccinations are given primarily to children. We vaccinate children for a variety of reasons: their growing immune systems are inherently highly susceptible to disease; some of the most infamous childhood diseases, like polio, can have lifelong, life-changing serious effects; many children spend most of their time in close proximity to other children in school and childcare situations, making them key vectors of disease; and the state maintains extensive control over that population through the requirements for school entry. Third, and most importantly, vaccines are most effective when the maximum number of people possible in a community are vaccinated, something called *herd immunity* or *community immunity*. Community immunity creates the central tension in vaccination controversy. Allowing voluntary nonvaccination diminishes the effectiveness of the protection offered, even to those who are vaccinated, and puts those more vulnerable to disease at risk. Vaccines are not 100 percent effective, so even vaccinated people gain protection from the herd. More importantly, some people, such as people with compromised immune systems because of illness, age, or treatments like chemotherapy and other immune-suppressing drugs, entirely rely on the community protection that vaccination provides to keep them healthy.

With vaccination, individuals always assume a little bit of risk in hopes of protecting others and themselves. Many vaccine proponents note that vaccinations carry risks just like any medication does, which is true. However, risk works differently with vaccination (Hobson-West; Casiday; Davis et al.; Bond and Nolan). Vaccination is, in most cases, mandated by law while many other medicines are not, meaning that risks are often imposed upon individuals. There are no immediate or even short-term benefits for vaccination that we might associate with other medicines, like the alleviation of symptoms or something unintended like weight loss. The consequences of not accepting the medication are also quite different—whereas you might simply experience more intense symptoms if you don't take a decongestant when you have a cold, if you refuse a required vaccination (or do so on behalf of your child), you may lose access to your doctor, lose health benefits, or lose your job if your employer requires a vaccination. Mandatory vaccination policies put the needs of the whole over the individual, making vaccination inherently social and public, in addition to being private, insular, and scientific. Because mass vaccination is ultimately a function of policy, not of mere scientific power, vaccines answer to a wide range of public voices, needs, and objections. When vaccination is understood not as a private choice to be individually accepted or rejected but rather as a product of public control over individual health, the reasons and rationales for controversy surrounding vaccines become easier to see.

Researchers in a variety of fields have attempted to uncover all the different beliefs behind vaccine refusal, often in an attempt to invalidate or disprove specific concerns or counterarguments to vaccination. Often, this research works to analyze these beliefs in a way that further reifies assumptions of deficit-based thinking and obscures the nuances of vaccine concerns (Offit and Hackett; Gullion et al.; d'Alessandro et al.).[2] For example, Robert Jacobson, Paul Targonski, and Gregory Poland created a "Taxonomy of Reasoning Flaws" following a meta-analysis of articles from 1966 to 2006 that discussed parental beliefs concerning vaccination.[3] Citing as their exigence an "anti-vaccine movement" that "represents an ongoing, broad, and diverse set of groups and individuals who often share concerns based on a variety of shared misconceptions," the authors sought to clarify the precise mechanisms by which parents misconstrue the facts in ways that support antivaccination belief and practice (3146). For example, the authors argue that parents want "to find order and predictability in random data," have "difficulty in detecting and correcting biases in incomplete and unrepresentative data," and are eager "to interpret ambiguous and inconsistent data to fit theories and expectations." In addition, these parents engage in "wishful thinking and self-serving distortions of reality," are subject to "pitfalls of second-hand information and miscommunication, including mass communication," and have "exaggerated impressions of social support" for nonvaccination or delayed vaccination (3147). Such research reifies the notion that people who refuse vaccinations for

---

2. Eula Biss's *On Immunity: An Inoculation* and Mark Navin's *Values and Vaccine Refusal: Hard Questions in Epistemology, Ethics, and Health Care* also merit mentioning here. Biss's perspective is popular and Navin's philosophical, but both draw similar, deficit-based conclusions about vaccine concerns and those who express them, ultimately arguing that some combination of wrong thinking, improper risk calculus, or selfishness is to blame for vaccine concerns.

3. Poland and Jacobson (2011) published a later *NEJM* commentary based on these observations, where they describe antivaccinationists as

> ranging from people who are simply ignorant about science (or "innumerate"—unable to understand and incorporate concepts of risk and probability into science-grounded decision making) to a radical fringe element who use deliberate mistruths, intimidation, falsified data, and threats of violence in efforts to prevent the use of vaccines and to silence critics. (98)

themselves or their children are delusional, unintelligent, or both, unequipped for persuasion but not beyond compulsion.[4]

Other disciplinary approaches complicate such easy narratives about who refuses vaccines, why they are refused, and what remedies might work to address the issue. Researchers in the social sciences have long undertaken a more open approach, conducting qualitative research on a wide range of populations to understand their vaccination beliefs and how those beliefs develop. These studies have illuminated issues such as the perceived risks and benefits of vaccination (Hobson-West; Casiday)[5] and the evolution of antivaccination as a social movement (Blume). In particular, the perspectives offered in Melissa Leach and James Fairhead's *Vaccine Anxieties* articulate tensions across vaccine concerns in a global, primarily UK context. The sources of vaccination concerns include tensions surrounding the public's engagement with science and its power to shape social behavior and public policy; anxieties about the global and personal contexts inherent in vaccination; and the fact that vaccination is primarily administered to children. Jennifer Reich's *Calling the Shots* identifies vaccine skepticisms, hesitancy, and refusal as, in part, a product of "individualist parenting," which values neoliberal values such as individual expertise and "getting informed" over accepting the advice of experts and acting on behalf of the "greater good" (11).[6] Approaches from

---

4. I thank Rachael Graham Lussos for this skillful sentence.

5. Parental notions of risks and benefits are frequently examined in studies of vaccine sentiment and related decision-making as well. As Pru Hobson-West points out, understanding parental decision-making through the lens of risks and benefits oversimplifies the field of contexts within which parents form opinions and make decisions about vaccines. Instead, Hobson-West advocates conceptualizing vaccination decisions as made among a field of uncertainties. Hobson-West also argues that the risk-benefit means of understanding vaccination decisions leads to the (also unhelpful) increased calls for scientific literacy. Although "Children's Health and the Social Theory of Risk: Insights from the British Measles, Mumps, and Rubella (MMR) Controversy," by Rachel Elizabeth Casiday, overall accepts a risk/benefit way of evaluating vaccine behaviors among parents, Casiday's study argues for a more nuanced mechanism for evaluating and understanding how parents weigh risks and benefits overall. Casiday looks at parent risk perceptions through three theories of risk: cultural theory, risk society, and psychometric models of risk perception, focusing her analysis on the autism–MMR scare in particular. Casiday finds that parents perceive high consequences for their vaccination decisions, whatever those are: "getting this decision 'right' came to symbolise what it means to be a good parent" (1065).

6. This is just one such example of how social science and public health approaches have worked to improve and complicate easy understandings of the nuances of vaccine skepticism. Streefland et al. seek to describe how vaccination acceptance works in predictable patterns across a variety of populations worldwide; New and Senior found that incomplete immunizers were more likely to be uncertain about the safety of the conditions necessary for being vaccinated (in the case of their study's focus, against pertussis). Lyndal Bond and Terry Nolan's work concludes that vaccine perspectives are complex and involve a number of factors, including "risks of vaccines, diseases, and robustness of the child's health," and also notes that that familiarity with disease shapes perception of "control over risks or outcomes" for parents.

within history demonstrate the breadth and depth of skepticisms expressed outside contemporary contexts (Conis; Colgrove; Largent). Folklorist Andrea Kitta studies narratives of vaccine skepticisms with a goal of understanding how urban legends and myths respond and are responsive to larger cultural values about medicine, science, and the body. Some work within public health and medicine—namely Julie Leask et al.'s work—takes these nuanced understandings one step further, providing communication recommendations directly to health care providers. Together, these approaches offer a rich, diverse understanding, from many disciplinary perspectives, of why vaccination skepticism persists. Yet controversy remains, and rhetoric in particular is poised to move beyond analysis and into action, as the orientation of its theory and disciplinary objectives are focused not just on understanding situations as they are but positing discursive paths forward.

Moving one step beyond this rich social science tradition, I argue that vaccines are controversial for another key reason: the vaccine's material operation as an embodied medical technology. Vaccines are not just inert scientific objects that have significance only through what humans do with them; rather, they are things with an agency of their own that motivates and perpetuates discord. Therefore, a rhetorical approach to understanding and intervening in this controversy is a pressing need and possible path to amelioration. Specifically, this text argues that a material rhetorical approach that examines the material complexities of vaccines and the ways that they shape discourse is needed to open new opportunities for persuasion.

CONTENDING WITH MATERIALITY

In its simplest terms, the vaccine is a collective, material piece of equipment.[7] There is the hollow needle, attached to a syringe filled with serum, injected into the body through a plunger. Of course, the needle, the plunger, and the

---

7. Here, I am borrowing the notion of equipment from Graham Harman, who uses Martin Heidegger's notion of tools and tool-being in his book *Tool-Being*. More than simply "present-at-hand" (*vorhandenheit*), tool-beings look at objects as equipment—as things that are always part of a whole, or essentially plural (as Harman says, there is no such thing as "an equipment," but equipment either exists in pieces of the whole or the whole all together). This view of objects illuminates how objects are present-at-hand (identified through the as-structure) and ready-to-hand (as tool-beings) to each other as part of the way they relate to one another. Therefore, tool-being is more than a "linguistic network or culturally coded system of 'social practices'" that transcends human praxis and looks at the "brutal subterranean realm" within which objects exist (Harman 4). In other words, tool-being refers to objects that exist within object-systems that connect to and dictate practices through the relation of objects within those practices. Focusing on the object shows the role that material things play not just in perceptions of activity, or as tools *through which we engage in the world, but in the actual*

syringe alone are not the vaccine—these are the delivery mechanisms for the serum, which contains the materials to vaccinate a body. Sometimes, the vaccine is the serum, made into mist, administered into the nose; in the case of rotavirus vaccine or in the parts of the world where oral polio vaccine is still administered, it is the serum, in a plastic tube, given orally. All this equipment works together to vaccinate. The serum itself is multiple and material as well, containing the antigen, an adjuvant, stabilizers, and preservatives, along with traces of antibiotics, cell cultures, and inactivating ingredients left over from the vaccine production process (Vaccines.gov). Once administered into a human, the serum fuses body and technology at a cellular level. The technology stimulates the immune system, which at once becomes modified by the technology and *acts as* the technology, as the immune system's artificial stimulation by the vaccine becomes the mode of protection from disease. The vaccine uses the body's operation to do its work, imbuing the body, as a system, with the capacity to fight disease.

Beyond such a cellular-level way of motivating human action, the vaccine creates human action in macro terms as well: vaccines facilitate relationships, injure bodies, emancipate the sick, configure the pace of diagnosis and medical practice, close off some communities, and open others up. Unlike with antibiotics or antidepressants or cholesterol-lowering drugs, the immunity that vaccinations confer ends up shaping human action beyond what the vaccine does in the body itself. Vaccines change the way we interact with others: who gets to go to school and who doesn't, how often immune-suppressing drugs can and should be prescribed, how often and for how long people are contagious. Vaccines affect the productiveness of a population and the vitality of a community. Vaccines keep systems running and run by healthy people.

Most significantly for a rhetorical understanding of vaccination, vaccines create and constrain conditions for discourse. From the injury in the arm at the site of the vaccination to global health imperatives, humans are in a constant state of responding to the exigencies created by vaccines. Humans might create the vaccine, humans might administer and receive the vaccine, and humans might imbue the vaccine's results with power. But once it leaves human hands, the vaccine itself is an independent operator, creating the conditions for discourse to occur and creating its own rhetoric as a material object.

---

operation, engagement, or doing of a reality. Such a perspective on vaccines as material objects is central to the analysis of vaccines as engaging material exigencies argued in this book.

Medical rhetoric, and related disciplines like the medical humanities, bioethics, rhetoric of science, and science and technology studies (STS) that grew before and alongside it, has long contemplated the role that material plays in constructing medicine and the scientific knowledge it is based upon. Interrogating science and medicine's treatment of material as self-evident and ideologically neutral is arguably one of the first and most prominent objectives of these disciplines, movements, and theories. The early rhetoric of science projects of Bruno Latour, Alan Gross, Deirdre McCloskey, and others challenged science's positivism and the material worlds that substantiated it, opening up science and the spaces that created scientific knowledge to social and rhetorical critique.[8] Research with similar objectives—Jeanne Fahnestock's *Rhetorical Figures in Science,* Leah Ceccarelli's *Shaping Science with Rhetoric,* and Sandra Harding's *The Science Question in Feminism,* among many others—expands and extends these ideas, critiquing the epistemological values of science and its insistence upon singular, stable, material realities. Similarly, scholars in the medical humanities have highlighted the ways that medicine has used the notion of a singular, stable reality to construct and produce pathological ways of defining bodies. Rebecca Kukla's *Mass Hysteria* unpacks the ideological investments of the technologies that pathologize what is actually the normal, embodied state of pregnancy; likewise, Bernice Hausman's *Mother's Milk* demonstrates how material structures, cultural values, and social norms constrain breastfeeding. Humanities and social science approaches to medicine demonstrate that scientific knowledge, though valuable, is not *the only* valuable way of knowing and making knowledge, applying the tools of critique to material associated with science, whether that material is a microscope, field notes, or an ultrasound machine.

Medical rhetoric extends these projects and investments from related disciplines, more specifically looking at documentation, argumentation, and language use, often to understand their persuasive qualities. In her 2005 foundational *Health and the Rhetoric of Medicine,* Judy Segal charts how disease is constructed rhetorically across places traditionally reserved for (capital *T*)

---

8. Specifically here, I am referring to work such as Bruno Latour and Steve Woolgar's *Laboratory Life: The Construction of Scientific Facts,* published in 1979. Other studies of the rhetoric of science have expanded on Latour and Woolgar's study by focusing on rhetorical analyses of scientific publications or the popular effects of scientific discoveries, such as Charles Bazerman's *Shaping Written Knowledge: The Genre and Activity of the Experimental Article in Science,* a historical study of publications of the Royal Society of London, and John Angus Campbell's analysis of Charles Darwin's rhetorical choices in *The Origin of Species* through a close reading of Darwin's published text as well as his journal writing. Across all these early texts, studies in the rhetoric of science examine how scientific information, which claims to be objective and non-rhetorical, is actually subjective and situational in many contexts.

Truth-making: patient charts, medical journals, and lab reports. Through analyzing narratives, language use, and metaphors to different rhetorical effect, the text engages in the process of critique by denaturalizing the material of medicine, calling into question its ability to constitute positivistic definitions of reality through its written objects and artifacts. Amy Koerber's *Breast or Bottle?* and *From Hysteria to Hormones,* Lisa Keränen's *Scientific Characters,* J. Blake Scott's *Risky Rhetorics,* and Jenell Johnson's *American Lobotomy* are just some texts that extend these observations and projects by accounting for the ways that scientific and medical concepts gain rhetorical power through language use across practice, policy, and reporting. These approaches offer invaluable insight and points of intervention into key questions in medicine and science by providing new understanding into how medical knowledge is produced; how voices and experiences are silenced amid dominant discourses; how material operates to reify dominant ideologies and blind professionals, often to the detriment of patients and communities; and how language persuades patients (that they are sick, should take a medication, should get a procedure).

As medical rhetoric and the rhetoric of health and medicine (RHM) have continued to expand, scholars have extended into new, embodied spaces in medicine and have developed new theoretical perspectives on material in health and medical contexts. Lora Arduser's *Living Chronic* offers one example of how RHM scholars are contending with reality, examining the lived experiences of patients with diabetes as they use the material of medicine to negotiate their bodies and experiences of disease. S. Scott Graham's *The Politics of Pain Medicine* takes on the materialist project most acutely, adopting perspectives from new materialism that aim to accept and understand materiality, studying discourses of physicians and practitioners who treat one of the most ephemeral of conditions—pain. Rather than critiquing the material X-ray as reifying hegemonic notions of bodies, how they are supposed to work, and how they shape patient experience in problematic ways, Graham makes an argument for material, accepting it as part of and constituting worlds and realities for patients and practitioners alike.[9] This move to understand how material works to create situations for rhetoric is also executed in Christa Teston's *Bodies in Flux,* where she examines the ways that material works to create and abate medical uncertainties across systems. In this purview, images are not just colonizing, fetishizing, hegemonic representations of bodies, as

---

9. Consequently, Graham outlines how discourse ontologizes pain: how it makes it material in ways that are essential to the practitioners who treat it and the patients who experience it, ultimately arguing that a "multiplicity of pain ontologies" coexist across the medical spectrum (35).

Kukla would conclude (105), but are rather constitutive, world-making objects with their own agency to shape situations. Teston concludes, "Medical images are more than representations that signify, represent, or are 'read' in a literary sense . . . they do more than they display" (52). Indeed, such perspectives are being taken up in studies of wearables (Gouge and Jones; Jack; Teston; Kessler), biohacking (Malatino), and genetics (Happe; Pender, *Being*, "Genetic Subjectivity") as well. Increasingly, RHM scholars explore spaces where materiality and subjectivity collide, and the objective of critique is not to denaturalize scientific material and uncover hegemonic forces guiding it but rather to expose its epistemological, ontological operation for how it brings knowledges and spaces into being.

Yet even existing material approaches to health and medicine weren't quite adequate for the problems and tensions that I kept uncovering in vaccination, and thus no existing rhetorical theory, concept, or principle alone would work to unravel the intractability of controversy surrounding vaccines. The problems of vaccine controversy don't seem to go away: the same arguments are exchanged, centuries apart; the same types of agents make the same types of claims that fail to persuade the same types of audiences; and clashes between the power of the state and personal choice continue to be rehearsed as new vaccines are adopted and vaccine mandates passed. If a rhetorical intervention is to provide lasting insight into these arguments, a new theory that accounts for that intractability, by considering the materiality of vaccination, is needed to better explain the discord and find new paths to persuasion amid disagreement.

CONSIDERING VACCINE RHETORICS: A THEORY OF MATERIAL EXIGENCE

Vaccination controversy is a unique site rhetorically—and therefore requires new theory-building—because it isn't quite the same phenomenon as other issues taken on by scholars in RHM and related fields. Although many projects in rhetorical studies examine controversial issues that involve diverse stakeholders and actors across situations,[10] no other controversy includes the requirement that nearly every single person on the entire planet engage in a singular, material, embodied experience at least once in a lifetime. Such

---

10. Most significant among such examples is J. Blake Scott's analysis on the rhetoric of AIDS. *Risky Rhetorics* offers perhaps the closest study of a controversy in health and medicine with the scope, intensity, and public health complexities as vaccination, but obviously covers a controversy with different populations, political inflections, and historical trajectory.

a scenario imbues vaccination with a unique set of rhetorical requirements that, when left unacknowledged and unaddressed, fuels only controversy and disagreement.

No comprehensive, book-length study of vaccination controversy has been conducted by a scholar in rhetoric. Bernice Hausman's *Anti/Vax* offers the most comprehensive examination of vaccination controversy from a humanistic perspective while delving less particularly into its rhetoric. Recent rhetorical treatments of vaccination have demonstrated how various facets of the issue work, primarily by understanding discourse and forms of argumentation. This research has demonstrated how vaccine skepticisms are articulated at the local level in response to flu vaccine (Lawrence, Hausman, and Dannenberg; Hausman et al.); the efficacy of website communication about vaccinations (Grant et al.); the complexities of flu vaccination for college students (Lawrence, "Healthy Bodies, Toxic Medicines"); and how notions of immunity operate among skeptical publics (Hausman, "Immunity, Modernity"). Beyond this work, other rhetorical treatments of vaccination controversy have examined particular parts of the controversy, such as the rhetorical work of the Wakefield study and the role that hedging played in articulating Wakefield's fraudulent findings about connections between MMR and autism (Kolodziejski), how Gardasil vaccine information works to attenuate risks and benefits (Malkowski), how mothers use rhetorical tactics to build arguments for and against vaccination (Carrion), and how epidemics and outbreaks generate new calls for vaccinations (Scott et al.). This work all reveals important facets to vaccination controversy in key ways by identifying and examining discourses and understanding how arguments operate, but none of them offer a rhetorical explanation for why controversy persists in light of hundreds of years of arguments and counterarguments.

To develop a paradigm for examining and explaining vaccine controversy and to move toward more productive modes of communication, I return to a slightly old and more than slightly contested concept—exigence—and reconsider it within a new materialist perspective.

Lloyd Bitzer's original formulation of rhetorical situation posited that rhetorical situations comprise an audience, constraints, and exigence, the latter of which he conceptualized as an "imperfection marked by urgency; it is a defect, an obstacle, something waiting to be done, a thing which is other than it should be" (6). Exigence, in Bitzer's original sense, was something that was shared by audience and speaker and could be modified by discourse; situations were not rhetorical if modification through discourse was not possible. Despite the many subsequent critiques of Bitzer's original concept (Vatz; Miller; Biesecker), the field of rhetoric's continued interest in and extensions of the model (Edbauer; Rice; Hunsaker and Smith; Smith and Lybarger) demonstrates how it can be a generative lens for understanding persuasive discourse despite some shortcomings in the original formulation. Specifically, Jenny Rice's notion of rhetorical ecology offers a significant rethinking of rhetorical situation as an interpretative paradigm for public discourse, extending the notion of rhetorical situation to "rhetorical ecology" as a framework for seeing how rhetoric works in public spaces.[11] Rice acknowledges that although rhetorical situation offers an important explanatory model "for thinking of rhetoric's contextual character," rhetorical situations "fall somewhat short when accounting for the amalgamations and transformations—the spread—of a given rhetoric within its wider ecology" ("Unframing" 20). Consequently, Rice's theory of rhetorical ecology accounts for the "issues of cooptation, and strategies of rhetorical production and circulation" that she argues are missing from a rhetorical situation paradigm (20).

I argue for another extension of the concept of rhetorical situation, one that expressly accounts for the material qualities of exigencies, to allow us to see rhetorical situations in new ways that create new opportunities for rhetorically informed persuasive responses. Theories of new materialism make such a renewed take on exigence possible.

New materialism accounts for the degrees to which objects and matter operate productively and with agency in the human world. By decentering the role that the human plays in making meaning, these perspectives account for the ways in which human actions—and rhetorics—are created and constrained by matter. This approach moves the notion of exigence in some ways back toward Bitzer's notion of exigence as having observable, factual components while decoupling materiality from a positivist paradigm and acknowledging the constructedness of situations (11). Such a rereading retains the explanatory power of the rhetorical situation, which examines how various speakers come together, what their discourses aim to do, and what happens when they interact, while accounting for the ways these interactions are still constructed and constrained by matter and are distributed across other speak-

---

11. These notions are outlined in "Unframing Models of Public Distribution: From Rhetorical Situation to Rhetorical Ecologies" and in her more recent *Distant Publics: Development Rhetoric and the Subject of Crisis*.

In making this argument, Rice is referring not just to the rhetorics and discourses that might occur in one rhetorical situation at one time but rather to those that cross situational boundaries, those that occur over time and space, and those that have a "viral spread" within a situation's ecology, be it a movement, a city or location, or an ideology ("Unframing" 19). Moreover, the rhetorical ecologies paradigm helps scholars in rhetoric "begin to recognize the way rhetorics are held together trans-situationally, as well as the effects of trans-situationality on rhetorical circulation" (20).

ers, space, and time. Namely, Bitzer's assertion that exigencies cannot be modified if they are not mutually comprehended is important here; an exigence that is not known cannot be changed. Such an impasse becomes simply intractable without accounting for exigence's material qualities and contending with them through discourse.

What does it mean to contend with an exigence's material qualities? More and more, the implications of the material world and how we understand it are brought to bear on individuals, from laws and policies that determine what chemicals are allowed into our air to assessing the long-term geological impact of practices like fracking and oil drilling. Questions at the intersections of scientific knowledge, material concern, and cultural consequence permeate various aspects of public life. As this happens, a cultural critique of these practices has proved to be, in Diana Coole and Samantha Frost's terms, increasingly "inadequate for thinking about matter, materiality, and politics in ways that do justice to the contemporary context of biopolitics and global political economy" (6). Culturally constructed or not, "the real," this perspective insists, must be contended with since materiality is productive and resilient, and so corresponding criticism examines how the real "exhibits agency," concerns "the status of life and the human," and connects to "broader geopolitical and socioeconomic structures" (7). Although these issues are attended to by the cultural constructivist perspectives first developed in the social construction of science, STS, and rhetoric of science movements, new materialism gives "materiality its due, alert to the myriad ways in which matter is both self-constituting and invested with—and reconfigured by—intersubjective interventions that have their own quotient of materiality" (7).

Material exigencies, as conceptualized here, are the exigencies created by material—imperfections marked by urgency that are inaugurated by central material objects that configure and demand discursive response. In the case of vaccination controversy, the material object is the vaccine itself along with its accompanying material. Not merely socially created or constructed, material exigencies demand discursive reactions from the human actors who must respond to the ways that objects act in the world—shaping professions, populations, environments, and bodies. As material, these exigencies cannot simply be ignored; they persist, even if actors fail to comprehend and acknowledge them, continuing to exert influence across situations and discourse, demanding response, and producing discord if those needs remain unaddressed. The orientation of this paradigm to the operation of large, lasting public controversy on a topic related to science and medicine is something that differentiates the notion of material exigence from other, related materialist theories and conceptualizations of the relationship between humans and matter, such as those reflected in Bogost's procedural rhetorics of software, Haraway's cyborg, ANT's agential objects, or Hayles's cybernetic bodies (Mara and Hawk 4–6).[12] A materialist approach to exigence (1) conceptualizes the material world as agentic and productive on its own, (2) accounts for how matter might have rhetoric across the situations in which humans debate, and (3) aims to understand how matter can generate imperfections that might be modified by discourse in contexts of particularly contentious public discord. In other words, although Bitzer's modernist perspective might have unnecessarily insisted on a "real" at the expense of the constructedness of situations, we can instead acknowledge constructedness as occurring not in place of, but as a result of materialities that motivate and must be contended with in rhetorical situations.

Material exigencies shape the discourses of vaccine controversy in some distinct ways. The following excerpt from an interview about flu vaccine offers an apt example of how to understand arguments about vaccination when viewed as responding to material exigence:

> And I'm just like, I wonder what's going on . . . So what is the, what are the long-term effects of the vaccine? How will people react to it? Will people be more dependent on it? Are there any other diseases that could potentially be caused off of this vaccine? . . . We would have to find out. Could it be cancer? You know, could it be, you know, it will all have to be based on what chemicals are inside. We would get something injected in us; we don't know what's in it. You know what I mean? So, it's uh, it's one of those tough things. Everybody's saying "Get this, get this. It's good for you." Is it though? You know, like, what's in it? You know. "Just a little bit of sugar." "Yeah, it'll be fine. It'll be fine." . . . Right, but what are the long-term effects of it? You know, that's what I get curious about. (Interview 7)

This participant—a father of three young children—articulates a range of anxieties as they relate to the operation of the vaccine and the embodied consequences of being vaccinated. First, he states an often-repeated concern

---

12. I borrow many of these distinctions, particularly those on Haraway, ANT, and Hayles, from the 2010 article "Posthuman Rhetorics and Technical Communication," by Andrew Mara and Byron Hawk. This article, as an introduction to a special issue of *TCQ* on posthuman rhetorics and technical communication, outlines a wide range of paradigms for conceptualizing the posthuman complexities of human–material interaction specifically in the context of technical communication and greatly shaped my thinking on the distinctions between these concepts—and their relative limitations to the problems of vaccine controversy and its material operations—and what I am proposing with material exigence here.

about vaccine ingredients—what else is in vaccines that we do not know about (sugar, chemicals)? Leading out of this concern, he connects that uncertainty to other, unintended consequences of the vaccination for his child, like other diseases and even cancer. And then finally he points to a trend across concerns about flu vaccine, further discussed in chapter 4, about larger, population-wide vaccine efficacy—problems like a body's dependency on the vaccine and increasing viral resistance and mutations to respond to the vaccine.[13]

All these concerns emerge out of the central, embodied material statement: "We would get something injected in us; we don't know what's in it." Here is a clash of material: the injection of something into the body that is ultimately perceived as unknown and beyond the scope of one's individual knowledge and ability to control. One might be tempted to say, "Well, we *do* know what else is in vaccines—ingredient lists are available on package inserts and online, and these ingredients have been tested for safety." But to respond as such ignores the materiality of the argument. He is not stating a simple question or revealing a basic ignorance of vaccine ingredients; rather, he is reacting to the range of concerns that emerge out of the embodied experience of being vaccinated, having a needle pierce skin and muscle, and having a substance injected that is ultimately unknown to him. What am I putting in my body? Does it have unknown or unintended consequences? Is what you are telling me about its benefits and risks and minimal potential for harm true—or necessarily the case *for me?* Will this vaccine protect or threaten my health? Those questions are motivated *by* and *through* the action of the material object on and in the human.

Although some of these questions might be answered with facts or data, the answers probably still wouldn't convince this person to vaccinate, because such a response does not address the material exigence that the vaccine creates, in this case the exigence of the unknown (further discussed in chapter 4). As nonhuman actors, vaccines create embodied, visceral concerns about what medicine can (and should) do to the body (Johnson "'A Man's Mouth'"). As such, the "imperfection marked by urgency" for the exigence of vaccination for this participant cannot be resolved by listing the ingredients in a vaccine. The exigence can be modified only by addressing the perceived irrevocable, unknown consequence or injury that will be brought to bear upon his body

13. Similarly, in the survey study reported on in the 2014 article "Healthy Bodies, Toxic Medicines: College Students and the Rhetoric of Flu Vaccination," participants reported "long-term, far-reaching uncertain effects" as a rationale for not vaccinating. For example, as quoted in that article, a sample response of such an argument was, "I believe that flu vaccines perpetuate the ever-evolving virus and if people who are otherwise healthy are getting the vaccine regularly, they are putting themselves at risk for a new epidemic that cannot be predicted of having the virus mutate with another species strain" (430).

or the bodies of his children if he vaccinates. In the examination room, faced with the demand to vaccinate, is unlikely the time and space for such persuasion to take place given the multifaceted ways in which such an exigence operates and the power that the fear and uncertainty provoke in shaping the argument provided here.

Reading the participant's description of these concerns about flu vaccine, it is easy to imagine the exigencies of disease to which a doctor might be responding when approaching this person about a vaccination: rates of flu in the community, the risk of flu being transmitted to a pediatric cancer patient in the practice, or high rates of flu morbidity and mortality that year. That practitioner might also reflect on personal experiences where seemingly healthy children and adults were quickly overcome by flu, requiring hospitalizations and even resulting in fatalities that were devastating and unexpected. This response, too, emerges out of the material qualities of vaccination and agency of the vaccine. Reducing cases of disease and viruses circulating in a community alleviates personal and professional concerns about the health of communities, leading to the promise of a post-eradication world without infectious disease. Across the rhetorical situation, these material exigencies are real, are active, and, if not comprehended and addressed, will remain unresolved.

This book examines four primary exigencies—disease, eradication, injury, and the unknown—that are particularly important to understanding the intractable nature of vaccine controversy. These exigencies are the imperfections, the "thing waiting to be done" that vaccines create, that must be further understood and addressed by corresponding material measures if real persuasive efforts can be reclaimed across the controversy. The analyses in this book examine vaccination controversy through this lens, identifying and accounting for the ways in which vaccines shape, constrain, and configure human action. Each of these exigencies is material insofar as it is enacted through material objects—the vaccines themselves—yet is also material in that it is enacted on complex objects systems—bodies, professions, families, and communities. Each analysis aims to demonstrate how, as material operates as an agent across the controversy, rhetorics become increasingly fraught as exigencies go unacknowledged, unaddressed, and unmodified over time.

The concept of material exigence within a material rhetorical framework *contribution* can be helpful for scholars in RHM in particular as we examine large, public controversies involving health, medicine, and science. Understanding an issue's material exigencies requires that researchers see discourses produced about medicine—particularly discordant discourse—as more than just "anti" or denialist, but rather as a particular way of responding to the exigencies that material in health and medicine create. A materialist understanding of risks and benefits, safety and harm, and health practices generally forces researchers to reconceptualize public responses to medical and health interventions (Pender *Being*). If we think of skepticisms not as simple deficit, a product of subscribing or not subscribing to the hegemony of science, or of "delusional thinking," but rather as a broader acknowledgment of the multiplicities of exigencies that are created by medical interventions, then rhetoricians can produce the nuanced methods of research, engagement, and intervention needed to reclaim persuasion and discourse within such issues. Resulting research and findings lead not toward a feigned neutrality, nor one of blind advocacy for unheard voices, but rather toward a radical form of understanding, one that aims to value and equalize positions that various publics might take toward science and science-based policy and practice. Examining material imperfections marked by urgency created by material also responds to calls for understanding the particular embodied experiences of individual subjects as we traverse medicine (Melençon; Gouge).

Finally, and most significantly for rhetoric, understanding material exigencies gives scholars in rhetoric a lens for refocusing analytical attention back to the exigencies of situations and the spaces where rhetoric can reopen opportunities for discourse. In the case of vaccine controversy, the four material exigencies discussed in this book operate as limits—realities that must be comprehended by rhetors if any progress is going to be made by discourse. These exigencies become open to modification only once they are fully acknowledged and understood as a first step and are matched with new, material responses in corresponding attempts at persuasion. Such a process allows controversies, like those surrounding vaccination, to regain their rhetoricity, revealing opportunities for persuasion and recovery of deliberative modes of rhetoric.

ABOUT THIS BOOK

Vaccine Rhetorics argues that material exigencies shape and constrain human action in ways that complicate rhetoric and facilitate controversy. This book uses the case of vaccination in particular to examine how material exigencies work and looks for what available means of persuasion might remain in such a contentious material context.

The rhetorical approach to understanding vaccination controversy in this book shows that existing ideas about vaccination skepticism reify what has been an unhelpful binary of conflict: doctors want to vaccinate patients out of some combination of professional hubris, blind trust in the scientific reasoning behind vaccination, and perhaps collusion with government and pharmaceutical companies; and parents and patients are skeptical about vaccines because of Jenny McCarthy, popular yet unfounded myths circulated about vaccination perpetuated by pseudoscientific and denialist theories, an inability to truly understand the scientific method or the statistics of a risk-benefit calculation, or a simple—yet immature and unthinking—desire to not be told what to do by a doctor or "the government." Recalcitrant, unbending, and insensitive, these actors clash and collide in conflict, unable to find common ground. Such perspectives also uphold the need for compulsion in lieu of persuasion, casting those who question vaccines as unreasonable, ignorant, and unpersuadable.

The analyses in *Vaccine Rhetorics* show that it's all more complicated and complex, laden with nuanced argumentation. A rhetorically informed persuasive approach to vaccination maintains that only by accounting for the full context of vaccination controversy, being attentive to its discourses, acknowledging the limitations of current responses, and crafting new ones that respond to people's concerns can resolution be possible. In place of such a characterization of vaccination controversy, this book re-examines vaccination itself as a material practice, involving needles, serums, and related equipment to facilitate their administration. Vaccines are material, as are the diseases that vaccinations protect against, the bodies that vaccinations act upon, and the spaces in which vaccinations occur. Looking at the controversy not as a series of arguments that keep clashing but instead as a series of material with their own rhetorics that create the conditions for discord shifts understanding of the persuasive options available to human actors who might aim to persuade in this context.

In the situations and data sources discussed in this book, the analysis shows precisely how a vaccine's material rhetoric operates in a situation to create the conditions for discord and how existing arguments emerge as inadequate for addressing situational exigencies in light of that understanding. Finally, each chapter considers how researchers in the rhetoric of health and medicine—as well as those in closely related fields or with adjacent research or practical objectives—might intervene and connect with stakeholders when informed by such a rhetorical understanding.

Chapters 1 and 2 explicitly examine how professional concerns evolve around material exigencies and vaccination. Chapter 1 analyzes the arguments made by doctors about vaccines in a small study of physicians, finding that vaccines motivate arguments about professional practice within material exigencies of disease aimed to prevent, treat, and cure. Chapter 2 examines the material exigence of eradication through an analysis of vaccination policy and public health, specifically looking at the 2014 outbreak of measles stemming from exposure at Disneyland. This chapter takes a wider view of material exigencies to understand how vaccines shape the exigencies of infectious diseases, with the goal of eradication (wherein even one case of a disease is unacceptable) driving policymakers. Chapters 3 and 4 focus on two sets of public stakeholders in vaccine controversy—parents and patients. Chapter 3 examines parent and patient discourses on the internet, using the case of vaccine injury confessionals as a site where parents use rhetorics of presence, leveraging the power of confession to respond to the exigence of injury. In chapter 4, interviews with adults about flu vaccines demonstrate how vaccines create unknown exigencies, embodied consequences of techno-scientific interventions that reify and react to the uncertainties of science and medicine itself. These analyses are meant to examine and highlight key spaces, agents, and stakeholders across vaccination controversy; I do not mean to say that vaccines *only* create material exigencies of disease for doctors, or that only hesitant parents respond to injury. Indeed, many parents respond to the vaccine's power to eradicate a disease like measles most prominently, and physicians express a wide range of skepticisms about the uncertainties of particular vaccines. Rather, I argue, material exigencies are always present and operational in a situation. They might be more or less exigent for different speakers depending on the specifics of the situation, its audiences and speakers, and constraints at play. The point of these analyses, therefore, is to demonstrate how material exigencies—and failure to comprehend and modify them—generate, motivate, and sustain discord across the issue and its rhetoric.

Each chapter works through the operation of material exigencies as creating and confounding vaccine debates while also demonstrating how nuanced, complex, and multifaceted the issue and experience of vaccination is across a wide range of discourses and actors. In the research for this book, I spoke to individuals who were ardent supporters of vaccination as well as those who had varying forms of skepticisms; the text-based media and online forums reported on here reflect this range of arguments as well. Also important is that these concerns span the entire vaccination schedule. There are parents who worry about the necessity of the birth dose of hepatitis B, physicians who insist that parents not skip Hib vaccine in infants, teenagers convinced that Gardasil is unsafe, and adults who question the necessity of flu vaccine. This research demonstrates that disease- and vaccine-specific skepticisms exist well beyond the debunked MMR–autism connection that gets the most media attention. Opening up the complexity of vaccination controversy is not just important for understanding the issue writ large but also fulfills a key rhetorical requirement of audience understanding that must be fulfilled if any real discursive study or intervention is to take place.

The work and perspectives presented in this book offer researchers in the field of rhetoric, and RHM scholars in particular, a material rhetorical approach for intervening and examining controversies in science and medicine that might help to improve discordant discourse in all its forms, from examination rooms to school boards to the floors of legislatures to the internet. This improvement happens by using rhetoric's analytical and productive capacities to better understand vaccine hesitancy and support, to account for exigencies and constraints, and to change rhetorics in public spaces to be open to deliberative forms of engagement rather than getting stuck in forensic or epideictic ones. Such an intervention also requires that rhetoricians of health and medicine make further efforts to understand the role that materiality plays in facilitating discordant spaces around science, medicine, and health in the public sphere.

In pursuit of such an intervention, this book demonstrates that (1) vaccination arguments and practices exist along a spectrum, from support to refusal, and that many rational, reasonable people actually exist along the middle of that spectrum; (2) public discourse must move away from existing stalemates and "pro versus anti" vaccine stances; and (3) a material rhetorical approach can generate a more nuanced model for understanding what vaccine skepticisms are, why they exist and persist, and what the available means of persuasion might be.

A FINAL NOTE ON MATERIALITY

I also want to make a final note about materiality and the data sources in this book. I realize that in most cases in this book, I am analyzing and understanding material rhetorics through the discourses about them, looking at how, upon analysis, they work according to the actors involved in the debate. So, I'm not always looking at material but rather tracing responses to material through discourse about it.

A reasonable response might maintain that this is inadequate—that material needs to be studied and understood as material only through a praxiographic study, like that advanced by Annemarie Mol, which actually attends to material objects, tracing them as physical objects through each space in which they operate. In light of this available critique, I offer two rationales for conducting a material study through discourse.

First, understanding the human articulation of material offers an important view of how that material rhetoric operates. Indeed, as I state above, it was my early interviews with physicians that first showed me, as a researcher, the connection to material, since the stories that doctors told me, it seemed, were laden with material that worked so heavily to mold every available course of human action. I often saw and experienced this material myself when I conducted the interviews, which were punctuated by the sounds of babies screaming after a vaccine, and conducted around and near refrigerators that stored doses of vaccines, orchestrating my own path through their offices (waiting in "well" waiting rooms separate from sick children on the "other" side, sanitizing my own hands before and after our interviews, etc.). More importantly, and as chapter 1 discusses further, it is in some ways impossible to read anything but material in discursive accounts of practices. In this sense, the discursive functions as a key way of understanding material, even if it is filtered through the human.

Second, material that facilitates debate in big, public issues is often not the same kind of material that can be followed in quite the same way as is the case in other instances. Mol can follow a specimen as it is examined by the pathologist to understand how the microscope ontologizes disease, but population-wide health concerns are not so specific and finite. They occur within and are facilitated by material across time and space, casual and clinical encounters, through methods of transmission and by viruses, bacteria, fungi, or other matter that we don't even always fully understand. If the ways in which material rhetorics shape the big problems in our world are to be contended with, a means is needed to account for those rhetorics that can't always correspond to a finite physical, praxiographic methodology and instead require researchers to turn to discourse as the artifact adequate for understanding materiality. Therefore, in this sense, this text offers such an alternative and demonstrates the value and utility of material rhetorical study through discursive analysis.

Vaccine Rhetorics examines vaccination as a material practice out of which the social and discursive emerge. Only by beginning with understanding how material shapes and constrains discourse can we truly understand the nature and construction of vaccine rhetorics—arguments of concern and support as they are expressed and experienced. This material rhetorical approach offers new explanations for centuries-old discord that still vexes vaccine proponents. The result of the analysis leads not to finite solutions aimed at persuading a hesitant public but toward a rationale for retaining persuasion in vaccination through a rhetorically informed approach to persuasion and modifying rhetorical situations. Overall, therefore, the goal of this text is to offer rhetoricians a framework for understanding materiality in the face of constantly changing, dynamic situations and controversies in science and medicine, like those presented by vaccine controversy, and a set of perspectives and methods for intervention as rhetoricians reach out into real spaces and problems in the public sphere.

CHAPTER 1

Doing Disease

DOCTORS LIVE and work in a world full of disease—common, uncommon, curable, incurable, mysterious, life-threatening, preventable. Therefore, in many medical practices, and certainly in most pediatric practices, the physician's primary task is to help a patient avoid the entrapments of illness by pursuing and maintaining health. When it comes to infectious disease, avoiding illness includes any number of things in addition to vaccination, from eating healthy foods to practicing basic sanitation.

Few of these preventive measures, however, carry the convenience and certainty of vaccines. They are administered once, in a doctor's office, health department, or other generally accessible site; side effects are typically minimal and mild; most people are eligible to get them; they are inexpensive (relative to other medical interventions and treatments); and life-threatening risks are literally one in a million. Following administration, those who are vaccinated are protected against some of the most significant, deadly diseases that have historically circulated. Vaccines change communities and change lives, with almost no uncertainty or risk.

Consequently, vaccination is a key preventive health practice for all medical specialties, particularly those involving the care of children and other groups at greater risk of communicable disease. In addition to preventing well-known deadly childhood diseases like polio, pertussis, and measles, which, when they were common, sickened and killed hundreds and in some cases thousands of children every year, researchers continue to explore vaccination as a means for preventing other troublesome diseases as well. Vaccines are currently being researched and developed against Streptococcus pneumoniae, malaria, and HIV/AIDS as well as noncommunicable diseases, such as cancers, type 1 diabetes, and celiac disease (Nossal). Beyond preventing diseases currently circulating, vaccination has the ability to shape disease trajectory and even eradicate diseases that are dangerous to patients and costly to health systems. Vaccination makes the world, but particularly the doctor's waiting room, safe for those most vulnerable to disease, like transplant patients and cancer patients, by preventing the most dangerous contagions. Vaccine skepticism concerns physicians and other vaccine advocates because it threatens the power of vaccination at a very basic level. If herd immunity is not maintained, diseases like measles or whooping cough, they fear, will run rampant in communities, risking serious complications and death particularly among those most vulnerable.

qualitative

The findings that emerged across my interviews with eight physicians indicate how understanding the material exigencies of vaccination sheds new light on why vaccines are controversial, specifically through the role of *disease* as a material exigence, which is the topic of this chapter. In these interviews, the value of vaccination was expressed through the vaccine's relationship to disease and the resulting relationship of those diseases to the physician's specialty, his or her typical treatment population, and related disease experience. This chapter examines how vaccine exigencies—and specifically the exigencies of disease—shape the rhetorical and professional contexts of doctors and ultimately professional practice. Understanding the vaccine not as a simple preventive measure but rather as a physical object with the ability to modify disease heightens and refocuses the role that vaccines play in the professional practices of doctors and thus demonstrates how powerfully disease operates as material exigence to constrain discourse concerning vaccines.

There are at least three reasons for examining physician discourses, primarily of vaccine support, as a starting place for understanding vaccine controversy. First, it is at the level of the doctor–patient interaction that this controversy can be felt most acutely; as discussed further in chapter 2, although vaccine mandates work for older children by controlling vaccination practices required prior to school entry, individual practitioners are often responsible for ensuring that vaccine recommendations are followed through infancy, when vaccines are often most critical. Second, and consequently, physicians mediate the primary space where exigencies of disease are articulated, as I argue that doctors ontologize vaccine-preventable diseases in their practices through vaccination. Third, examining physician discourses through the lens of materiality attempts to subvert dominant narratives about the sources of vaccination controversy, shifting explanation for discord away from parent ignorance and toward addressing the larger rhetorical situation surrounding vaccination, including understanding disease as a material exigence that drives the professional constraints of doctors, revealing the ways that discourses become constrained by material exigencies.

In this chapter, I first discuss how material exigencies of disease operate in vaccine controversy, using Annemarie Mol's notion of ontology-in-practice to argue that vaccines are a way for doctors to do disease through the crucial task of prevention, thus making them key professional objects. Then, I examine themes across the physician interviews conducted for this research, looking broadly at how disease operates in their discourses and how vaccines are configured as objects that help them to modify infectious diseases in their practices. The arguments and observations in this chapter, therefore, establish how material exigencies work to facilitate discord across vaccine controversy, beginning with the operation of disease as a material exigence in the professional practices of physicians.

MATERIAL EXIGENCE: VACCINES AND THE MODIFICATION OF INFECTIOUS DISEASE

Like many conditions and ailments addressed by medicine, infectious disease[1] functions through a series of material enactments and responses in medical settings (Teston *Bodies in Flux*). *Unlike* many other conditions, however, infectious disease is mediated through a range of visible, material certainties: the viruses and bacteria that cause infectious disease are things that can often be seen or detected; the body creates antibodies and other immune responses that can usually be assessed in some way; and the infection typically creates symptoms that can be detected, tracked, and treated. Compared with conditions like chronic pain, multiple sclerosis, or depression, which have multifactorial etiologies that can operate differently from patient to patient and may have no firm diagnosis or even measurable cause, infectious diseases operate (or seem to operate) with a degree of material stability. Infectious diseases are also some of the most accepted consequences of social life. The perceived seriousness of infectious disease increases through its ability to spread quickly within social settings, the invasiveness of its infection, and the evasiveness of

---

1. In this chapter, I am using the definition of infectious disease used by the Mayo Clinic as a disease caused by a bacterium, virus, fungi, or parasite; this definition allows the use of "infectious disease" that also includes communicable and noncommunicable diseases, since I did not think it was productive to draw those distinctions here (Mayo Clinic, "Infectious Disease").

cure.[2] As far as we know, other ailments, like diabetes, heart disease, and most cancers, all can be developed by a person on his or her own; infectious disease uniquely arises as people interact with things and with each other. Finally, the combinations of particular disease attributes—a disease with high morbidity, high mortality, and few effective cures—are material realities that will likely, within our modern system of public health and medicine, engage cascading systems of disease response and their related material consequences.

Also unlike other conditions treated by medicine, vaccines exist to prevent some infectious diseases, often so effectively that the vaccine is the only way that some diseases still exist in a physician's office. Most pediatricians in the US in the twenty-first century will never see a case of polio in their primary practice, for instance. They will not put a patient in an iron lung, will not monitor that child's (hopeful) recovery over days and weeks. They will not see numerous students from the same class or children from the same neighborhood fall victim to the same symptoms in rapid succession, like doctors often did in the 1940s (Oshinsky). But most pediatricians will recommend and administer the polio vaccine; some may even reject patients from practices because they refuse it. They might have extensive conversations with patients over the need for the polio vaccine despite the perceived remoteness of the risk. They will order it, store it, and complete paperwork that verifies its administration. They may even use it rhetorically, knowingly or unknowingly, as they post promotional materials for vaccines in their offices that use the dreaded iron lung as a tactic for demonstrating the importance and life-saving power of vaccines. However, the polio vaccine doesn't just prevent polio for the doctor recommending and/or administering vaccination. Rather, I argue, the polio vaccine *ontologizes polio,* materializing it as a disease with attendant risks to be prevented through the vaccine. Or, to use Annemarie Mol's terminology, vaccination is a way for doctors to *do disease*—to materially enact the disease as they manipulate and are manipulated by the tools designed to mediate it.

Polio is real—very real. But as diseases are ontologized through the material that responds to them, the vaccine is the primary way through which a disease like polio is still materially present in medical spaces (in the US, in the twenty-first century, of course). Consequently, doctors want to see similar fates for diseases like Hib, rotavirus, and, of course, flu, and they see vaccination as the linchpin in such efforts—they want to see a day when flu is as rare

---

2. Such are the premises of the health belief model, which asserts a number of factors that are predictive of whether a person will pursue preventive measures, like vaccination, or not. These factors include severity of and susceptibility to disease (Kloeblen and Batish); this is also further discussed in chapter 4.

as polio. Therefore, to refuse polio vaccine is not just to refuse that vaccine for that disease but also to reject a primary means of professional enactment, a way of *doing disease*. Understanding how vaccines operate in this way, as creating material exigencies of disease to be modified and addressed, offers key insight into why vaccination controversy can be so troublesome to physicians in particular and why discourse that patients exchange with them about vaccinations can be so intractable.

Ontologizing Disease

Mol theorizes how diseases are ontologized through the material practices of medicine in *The Body Multiple: Ontology in Medical Practice*. Mol analyzes the role that objects play in medicine, arguing that looking at objects as stable, passive things that are manipulated by different agents produces problematic analyses that tease out the different "perspectives" that people have on objects. Mol argues that such forms of analysis fail to account for how objects constrain or produce particular practices because they foreground human interaction with objects, eliding the ways in which the objects themselves act as agents. Mol says instead that objects are "things manipulated in practice." When one acknowledges the multifaceted operations that objects can signify in practice,

> reality multiplies. If practices are foregrounded there is no longer a single passive object in the middle, waiting to be seen from the point of view of seemingly endless series of perspectives. Instead, objects come into being— and disappear—with the practices in which they are manipulated. . . . The body, the patient, the disease, the doctor, the technician, the technology: all of these are more than one. (5)

Therefore, for Mol, when objects are analyzed as embedded figures in different practices, or as objects with ontologies in practice, the result is not a series of different perspectives on, interactions with, or contradictions to the object. Instead, objects are conceptualized as multiple, and realities are as multiple as the practices in which objects emerge from, engage with, constrain, or motivate human behaviors. In this sense, an object's "ontologies are brought into being. . . . they inform and are informed by our bodies, the organization of our health care systems, the rhythms and pains of our diseases, and the shape of our technologies" (6–7). The study of medical practice from this lens does not involve finding objects (whether they are diseases, medications, or X-ray machines) and then describing how those things are seen within different perspectives (from the perspective of patients, from the perspective of doctors, etc.). Rather, objects create multiple ways of doing disease as they create different enactments of disease response.

Mol also argues that diseases and the practices that intervene in them are bound to one another and are co-constitutive. In the case of atherosclerosis in the clinic she studies, plaque needs the microscope in order to be found, and plaque needs to be found to diagnose atherosclerosis (consequently, atherosclerosis needs the microscope to be ontologized as a disease). As a result, humans operate in coexistent, multiple realities because these "different enactments of disease entail different ontologies. They each do the body differently" as they interact with technologies in different ways across the system (176). These multiple realities guide the activities of doctors and patients; doctors and patients are positioned in separate spaces, with the patient as the shared object of discourse, but the inanimate objects in those systems are not just *seen* differently within the perspectives of the doctor and patient. Rather, they *are different objects* with different ontologies in separate realities. Mol also states, "Shifting from understanding objects as the focus point of various perspectives to following them as they are enacted in a variety of practices implies a shift from asking how sciences *represent* to asking how they *intervene*" (152 emphasis added). Using Mol's praxiographic method to understand an object's ontology-in-practice, the researcher must shift from seeing objects to following them as they are used in practices that do different things to bodies in the effort to achieve health or treat an ailment.

Such a perspective on material in medical practice offers a key starting point for understanding material exigencies as they motivate discourse—and discord—in large public controversies like those involving vaccines. In the case of the vaccine, following the vaccine through a physician's practice reveals the ways in which a vaccine functions as a nonhuman actor that acts with agency of its own upon humans, creating the conditions for and entrapments of disease response, and generating other objects, object-systems, and units of operation to further act upon humans to respond to the disease (Bogost).[3]

---

3. Here, I borrow the notion of unit operation from Ian Bogost's *Alien Phenomenology: Or What It's Like to Be a Thing*. Here, Bogost maintains that if we think of objects as units and their interaction as operations, then we can think of all things the way that object-oriented programmers think about the objects they create in a piece of software—all units are equal in that they are all packets of materials with a set of states and behaviors; they operate in conjunction with other, adjacent units, but they are always distinct, and entire worlds of meaning and possibility exist within the packet of meaning that is the object. In this sense,

> things are not merely what they do, but things do indeed do things. . . . Units are isolated entities trapped together inside other units, rubbing shoulders with one another uncomfortably while never overlapping. A unit is never an atom, but a

Perhaps most critically, such a view demonstrates the power of objects like vaccines to change and constrain doctors, professions, and diseases themselves. However, Mol's perspective alone cannot account for controversy and discord that erupts as these different ontologies and practices of doing intersect. Considering material rhetorics further allows us to see how rhetorics emerge around material in medical practice, and how material can constitute exigencies that demand response.

Material Rhetorics and Exigencies

Recent work in rhetorical studies has attempted to merge a consideration of materiality and rhetoric to understand how objects operate suasively in various contexts. One key way in which these relationships are conceptualized is Scot Barnett and Casey Boyle's notion of rhetorical ontology, wherein

> things are rhetorical, in other words. Understanding them as rhetorical, however, requires more than a leap of imagination; it requires a shift in some of rhetoric's most entrenched critical, methodological, and theoretical orientations. . . . Rhetorical ontology highlights how various material elements—human and nonhuman alike—interact suasively and agentally in rhetorical situations and ecologies. (1–2)

Barnett and Boyle's concept of rhetorical ontology offers a theory for "how to do things with things," wherein rhetoric as a practice moves away from a knowledge-making one that makes sense of the world as it relates to humans and toward one where objects are accounted for as operating with their own agency to which humans must respond and with constraints of their own. As specifically discussed here, material exigence as a concept builds upon this idea, accounting for the suasive actions of objects in order to understand how they motivate and constrain discordant discourse about objects in medicine.

---

set, a grouping of other units that act together as a system. . . . This is the heart of unit operation: it names a phenomenon of accounting for an object. It is a process, a logic, an algorithm if you want, by which a unit attempts to make sense of another. (Bogost 28)

Bogost argues that the project of ontology is to describe, analyze, and understand unit operation—to examine how realities emerge from the interaction of units through their operations. Units always remain separate and distinct, yet they are infinite in how they may operate.

In considering how the material exigence of disease operates, I offer the following hypothetical scenario of a case of measles to demonstrate the multiple ways that vaccines exert powerful influence in rhetorical situations involving humans, communities, and diseases, while also constraining discourse and producing opportunities for discord.

Let's say that a child is sick with a high fever and a rash; the parent might suspect a wide range of things are wrong and ultimately decide to bring that child to the doctor. Once the child's diagnosis is confirmed as *measles,* a series of unique material actions may be provoked: those who were in the office during and immediately following the appointment will be contacted and possibly quarantined and tested; public health interventions may begin to interview the child and the family regarding their whereabouts and possible exposures during periods of contagion; public alerts might be issued through local media to help identify anyone who might have been exposed; and even school or business closures are possible if needed to avoid further contamination and spread. The sick child will receive intensive care in hopes of containing the disease and avoiding the most serious of complications from the illness. With each new system that a disease engages, a new set of material follows, such as testing procedures and kits, forms and reports, medications and treatments, and personal protective equipment (PPE). As the disease moves beyond the immediate situation at the doctor's office, additional audiences and identities may be called into being in the resulting rhetorical situations. A healthy, thirty-four-year-old man who may be at Starbucks at the same time as that child may have no existing discourse available to him about vaccines or measles or even public health generally until faced with a situation where he needs to be tested for exposure to measles, accept an MMR booster, or contract the disease itself if he wasn't sufficiently immune to begin with. All of this response stresses the system, diverting attention from other public health matters, and still carries the uncertainties of disease in a community that may not be able to be contained or cured without complication.

All this happens because, as a vaccine-preventable disease, any case of measles, even just one, is too many. As diseases become vaccine-preventable, the apparatus for treating or curing them begins to dissipate, meaning that doctors must do them primarily through prevention. Doctors become less adept at quick diagnosis; parents don't know what the telltale signs of very serious illnesses look like and therefore may bring children into public spaces while they are contagious, which puts larger populations at risk. Thus, the vaccine functions at a critical moment in the biopolitical life of the infectious disease, demonstrating the vaccine's ability to modify and change disease not just for humans but for the disease itself as well. As the earlier example of polio demonstrates, polio is just as incurable now as it was before the first polio vaccines in the 1950s. More seasoned doctors constantly decry that newer doctors don't know how to recognize vaccine-preventable diseases that are increasingly less common because of vaccines, such as Hib, whooping cough, or measles. Once the disease becomes "vaccine-preventable," the vaccine is the primary mode through which doctors enact the disease. Therefore, other factors, like timeliness in diagnosis, funding for research for cures and treatments, and even training in and knowledge of symptoms and available treatment options, are rerouted to address other diseases of more pressing concern. There is simply no need for specialized equipment or knowledge of—and hence material for—highly uncommon or rare diseases. The importance of vaccines are articulated through discourses about their safety and efficacy and community benefit, but as a material object, the vaccine demands that human actors work to prevent disease, not just because that's the vaccine's chief job, but because the other equipment available to modify disease are ultimately inadequate by comparison.

Rhetorically, such a situation reveals how material shapes and constrains discourse—and in this case how disease specifically functions as a material exigence created by vaccines. Disease operates as a material exigence in vaccine controversy through the power that vaccines have to alter bodies, systems of disease response, social spaces and who gets to inhabit them, and disease itself. As objects of prevention, vaccine systems and equipment constrain the rhetorics and audiences that must respond to the exigence of disease. Discourses that fail to acknowledge or modify that exigence will produce discord as they do not fit within the material object constraints created by the vaccine. As a paradigm for analysis, therefore, material exigence highlights the spaces where objects act with agency on humans and identifies the ways that discourse becomes strained and constrained as rhetors fail to comprehend or modify those exigencies in rhetorical situations.

The doctors' interviews analyzed next demonstrate the ways that vaccines function as ways of doing disease—of calling disease into being and responding to it through the practice of medicine, deeply tied to personal experiences with different diseases; the diseases they had "seen" as physicians; and the affordances, limitations, and ethical responsibilities of their professional specialties.

DOCTORS DOING DISEASE:
VACCINATION IN MEDICAL PRACTICE

For this study,[4] I interviewed eight doctors in in the southwest region of a mid-Atlantic state (IRB# 605786) from 2012 to early 2013.[5] The participants reflect a convenience sample of physicians, recruited via email, personal contact, and willingness to participate. Members of the Department of Pediatrics in a local consortium of pediatrics practices received recruitment materials via email, and the four doctors who responded to the email solicitation were interviewed. The remaining four interviewees were recruited via snowball and friend-of-a-friend techniques, through professional contacts in the area.

The resulting interviews were conducted with a wide range of physicians having different practices, specialties, years of experience, and positions on vaccinations, as well as both male and female participants. Overall, I interviewed four general pediatricians, a pediatric oncologist, a pediatric infectious disease specialist, a family practice physician who is also the director of a public health district, and a doctor of obstetrics and gynecology (ob/gyn). The interview responses reflected some areas of distinct difference based on specialty but also some important areas of consensus as well.

The interviews were conducted in a semistructured format, designed to elicit natural conversation, covering a range of questions about the physician's overall background, position on vaccinations in general, and experiences with flu and flu vaccine in particular, as outlined in Table 1.

For purposes of this study, focusing on flu vaccine offered a wider view on vaccinations among a variety of populations, not just children and infants, and allowed physicians across specialties to discuss varying experiences with vaccinations and vaccine refusal. (Not all specialties administer childhood vaccinations, but all administer or encourage flu vaccine since it was recommended for all healthy adults over the age of six months old, which is still the CDC's recommendation at the time of this writing.) Interviews averaged 45 to 50 minutes and were conducted in a variety of locations—doctors' offices (when possible), doctors' homes, and an academic office at a university. The

---

4. Portions of these interviews are also analyzed in the 2018 "When Patients Question Vaccines: Considering Vaccine Communication through a Material Rhetorical Approach" in *Rhetoric of Health & Medicine*.

5. This study was initially conducted at Virginia Polytechnic Institute and State University under IRB Number 10-489; this IRB protocol expired after I left Virginia Tech. As I continued to analyze the data but did not do any new recruiting or gathering of data following that point, I obtained approval for continuing use of existing data at George Mason University in October 2013 to analyze the transcripts reported on here, which remains active as of this writing.

TABLE 1. Physicians' study interview questions

INTRODUCTORY/BREAK-THE-ICE QUESTIONS

Where did you attend college and medical school? When did you graduate?

How long have you been a doctor?

What specialty did you choose and why?

PROFESSIONAL BACKGROUND

Describe your current medical practice. How big is the staff? How many nurses and assistants are there? How long has this practice been open? How has it changed over time?

What is your role in the medical practice?

What, if any, professional organizations do you belong to?

VACCINATION EXPERIENCES

What are your positions on vaccinations? How important do you think they are?

How have vaccinations changed over time in your practice? Do you feel you give more vaccinations now than you did when you first became a doctor?

How do you talk with other members of your practice—including other doctors and nurses—about issues related to vaccinations? Do you feel these problems come up in staff meetings and evaluations? What issues/problems and remedies have you all discussed?

Does the staff undergo any special training or instructions on how to counsel parents on vaccinations? What procedures and processes are in place to ensure children are vaccinated properly and on time?

How much time would you say you spend in an average day, week, or month counseling parents on vaccination decisions? What do their concerns tend to be? How are they similar/different for each vaccine?

Are there particular vaccines that are questioned more than others?

What do you think about the questions parents ask?

What do you think would help make parents feel more secure about vaccines? Do you think your personal interaction with them and assurance about the safety of vaccines is convincing?

Where do you see your views about vaccinations within the medical field? Do you feel you are more or less strict about vaccinations than your colleagues?

How do you feel about the recent ACIP recommendations that expand flu vaccinations? Were you surprised by this change?

What do you see as the major benefits of flu vaccine? Are there any drawbacks?

Why do you think flu vaccination rates aren't higher?

What do you think doctors could do to facilitate conversations with patients about vaccinations? What resources would you like to see or use that you think could make those conversations easier?

doctor and practice names provided in Table 1 are pseudonyms to protect the anonymity of study participants.

These physicians reported that vaccination functions as a complex professional issue that affects all aspects of their practices, from the purchase and storage of vaccines, to the safety of their waiting rooms, to the insufficiency of the time they have to spend talking to parents about vaccines. They also demonstrate a wide range of ideas about which diseases are the most important to prevent in striking comparison to which vaccines they get the most questions about from parents. For all doctors, though, vaccines function as a critical professional tool, essential to the purpose of their jobs and the daily operations of their practice.

Overall, three themes related to the value of vaccination and disease exigence were expressed throughout the interviews. First, the benefits of vaccination, for doctors, stretched far beyond just the prevention of disease. Vaccinations assist with differential diagnosis, reduce the chances of secondary complications among patients who contract vaccine-preventable disease, and limit the use of antibiotics, which may cure infections at the expense of serious side effects to the patient and contributing to general antibiotic resistance and thus depleted treatment options overall. For these doctors, the value of the vaccine is deeply connected to the perceived severity of the disease it prevents. Their views are rooted in personal experiences with severe diseases in emergency rooms and hospitals, diseases that often resulted in injury or death for the patients. Second, disease severity varies based on perspectives linked to physician specialty and the risks associated with each disease relative to the patients they most commonly treat. And finally, other professional activities located in the context of the local community or individual practice also factor greatly in doctors' perspectives on vaccination. Local outbreaks of disease motivate increased attention to vaccinations among patients and practitioners and shape the importance of a vaccination relative to the contexts of the local area. Vaccinations also help ensure the safety and acceptance of immune-compromised patients to a practice, of which there are a growing number.

Disease and the Benefits of Vaccination

One of the most striking observations I had almost immediately after I began these interviews was that although I had contacted doctors to interview them about vaccinations, our conversations were chiefly about diseases—their relative severity, how they are treated, and the importance of preventing them. Each vaccine-preventable disease we discussed had different levels of risk associated with it based on the treatment options for the disease, its rate of fatality, and the populations the physician chiefly served in his or her practice. For example, some doctors were willing to admit that varicella (chickenpox) vaccine wasn't entirely necessary for some children and therefore was something they were comfortable with parents refusing or delaying. Meanwhile, other doctors described chickenpox as a deadly disease that could be fatal to immune-compromised children and adults.

I soon realized that, for these doctors, to talk about vaccination was really to talk about the best way to respond to disease. Diseases that could make a child very ill, very quickly, such as meningitis, were of the greatest concern to the pediatricians interviewed, for example. Meningitis is preventable by three vaccines that protect against meningococcal, Haemophilus influenza B (Hib), and pneumococcal infections, and these were often referenced in the interviews as "must have" vaccines that were nonnegotiable in pediatric care.

Such diseases needed to be prevented at all costs because the ramifications of contracting them included severe symptoms, few or inadequate treatment options, and high likelihood of disfigurement or death. Meanwhile, other diseases were acceptable for some because they were perceived as mild or treatable depending on the child's overall health and family situation (for example, if there was a parent or caregiver available to stay at home with a child who became ill with chickenpox, the need for chickenpox vaccine was not as acute). Such a phenomenon was most explicitly described by Dr. Lambda, a family practice doctor who is also director of a public health district, who articulated disease severity relative to each of the many different patients in her district—for a pregnant woman, it might be flu, whereas meningitis would be the biggest concern for an elderly patient traveling to a region where meningitis is endemic.

Doctors described a complex of factors in defining the seriousness of a disease. For example, although antibiotics can treat many of the infections that cause meningitis, they are limited in that they carry risks of additional side effects, and the disease must be diagnosed quickly for treatment to be effective. Yet, as described further in other physician interviews outlined below, Hib infection in particular presents with nonspecific symptoms that could appear to be any of a number of different viral or bacterial illnesses initially; only upon further, and more invasive, testing can Hib be confirmed. The vital time lost treating Hib contributes to its severity as well, as a child can become very ill, very fast, past a certain threshold. Furthermore, Hib and pneumococcal infections can cause a broad range of other ailments and complications, such as pneumonia and epiglottitis (CDC, "*Haemophilus Influenzae*"). According to the Children's Hospital of Philadelphia (CHOP), before the first Hib vaccine was licensed in 1985, about 20,000 children in the US developed "severe Hib disease" each year, with nearly 1,000 fatalities (CHOP). The pneumococcal vaccine administered to children today was licensed in 2000 and presently protects against thirteen strains of bacteria. By contrast, according to the CDC, incidents of Hib were .08 per 100,000 in children under five in 2015, and pneumococcal disease had decreased to 9 per 100,000 people from a previous rate of 100 per 100,000 (CDC, "*Haemophilus influenzae*," "Pneumococcal disease").

The Hib and PCV vaccines have not only reduced the number of infections and deaths; they have also changed the standard practices for diagnosis and treatment of children with fevers in pediatric practices. Dr. Zeta characterized the risks and treatment of Hib and pneumococcal infections pre and post vaccine as follows:

> Kids will have fever, maybe the younger kids don't feed well. Within 24 hours they can become comatose. So we spent a lot of time as residents evaluating kids who came in just with fever and no other reason, and usually it's just a viral illness, that's what we find now, but back then you didn't know: is this just another viral illness, or do they have early stages of Haemophilus or pneumococcal sepsis? And Prevnar, the pneumococcal vaccine, that's the other vaccine that's made a huge difference. So, we used to do a lot of blood work on kids, a lot of spinal taps on kids, under a year of age, coming into the offices or emergency rooms to make sure they didn't have occult sepsis or meningitis. So there's a lot of morbidity associated with kids coming in with fever. A lot of kids got hospitalized, to make sure they didn't have it, and that's all gone away, since vaccines. So our approach is very different to say a 1-year-old who has a fever now compared to what it was 20–30 years ago. Assuming that they've been vaccinated against these particular diseases.

Dr. Alpha, a pediatric infectious disease specialist who focused most of her career on treating pediatric AIDS patients, described similar experiences treating children prior to the introduction of vaccines that protect against meningitis. Overall, Dr. Alpha described the experience of diagnosing and treating meningitis before vaccinations as one characterized by uncertainty. In the case of children who presented with nonspecific symptoms, like high fevers that could be caused by a number of possible infections, the time spent determining a diagnosis was time inevitably not spent treating the disease itself. At the same time, once telltale signs of meningitis (such as spots on the extremities) were present, the child's risk of severe complications and death had increased substantially. Even with treatment, children could still have permanent repercussions from disease, such as lost limbs and heart conditions. She also described the experience as one dominated by a constant sense of responsibility for taking care of a child who presented with life-threatening symptoms:

> When we would be on call at night, we would see children come in with fever, and um, sometimes they would be crying because they were in pain or sometimes they were totally quiet and they were the scariest because they were so overwhelmed by an infection they didn't even cry . . . we were responsible for drawing up all the blood, doing all the spinal taps, and getting all the antibiotics in . . . We would literally push the antibiotic and then a steroid, you know, to try and get the antibiotic on board but minimize the inflammatory response, so you wouldn't have an overwhelming response that might make the child very sick.
>
> So, and sometimes it would be, or you would be in clinic and you would see u-uh a child out there and they were waiting to be seen and you might see little spots on that little child's hands and feet and you thought (finger snap) meningococcal meningitis, get that mom in here because you knew that child could have overwhelming sepsis and just die before you even get them to the hospital or survive with missing limbs or hands or, you know purulent fluid around their heart.
>
> And so y-you were just THERE and we were responsible, we had no protected hours, we could be on for 36 hours and you would be responsible for that child. A lot of times you didn't want to LEAVE because, you know, were trying to save that, develop the sense of responsibility for that child.

Drs. Alpha and Zeta describe a range of complications in the treatment of meningitis before vaccines were developed. Diagnosis was difficult, invasive, and time-intensive. Complications from meningitis develop quickly, with serious consequences. Even antibiotics needed to be administered with care to ensure that they didn't do more harm than good. However, after those vaccines were developed, Dr. Alpha reports, "now you can say, well, it's probably not [Hib]. It can almost help you with differential diagnosis." If a child is up-to-date on vaccinations and presents with a high fever, the number of possible diseases it could be is at least reduced, shaping the courses of action to diagnose and treat the potential ailment.

In both these cases, we can see how vaccines have real, tangible effects on the professional practices of doctors. Vaccinations fit into the complex situation not only by contributing to the prevention of disease in healthy children but also by greatly impacting the treatment of and response to sick ones in clinics and emergency rooms as well.

Disease Severity and Specialty/Subspecialty

Perceptions of disease varied based on perspectives rooted in physician specialty as well. The general pediatricians interviewed largely stressed that their jobs were to prevent disease—"to produce a healthy adult at the end of 18 or 21 years of care," as stated by Dr. Delta, a general pediatrician. However, maintaining health by limiting exposure to contagion functioned as a primary professional goal for other specialties, such as pediatric oncology. For Dr. Gamma, the pediatric oncologist I interviewed, her relationship to vaccines is shaped by how pediatric cancer constrains treatment options for her patients.

The consequences for Dr. Gamma's patients, should they contract any vaccine-preventable disease, are severe, and the grave concern she has for her patients was largely reflected in her vehement defense of vaccines. In contrast to the discussions I had with all the other doctors, chickenpox emerged early in the interview as a disease of significant concern, as opposed to Hib or pneumococcal meningitis. Later, as we discussed chickenpox more, Dr. Gamma explained that she had participated in early research for a chickenpox vaccine while at another research institution. This was an area of significant interest for her in particular, she stated, because it was a vaccine designed to help immune-compromised patients, like her cancer patients. Her characterization of the severity of chickenpox to pediatric cancer patients also explained the reason this vaccination was particularly important to cancer patients:

> I have people who fly on airplanes, and you realize your child has chickenpox, right? "Oh yeah." I said, well, you're not supposed to be flying. "Yeah, don't tell anybody." Yeah, really nice, so you know, the person sitting next to you has breast cancer? And they're in active therapy? Thanks. You know, they don't get that they can kill people doing this. . . . I just don't, people are not cognizant of risks they put others in. . . . So, I don't necessarily have any problems with exposing normal healthy children to chickenpox, although, of those, one of those children is going to have meningitis or overwhelming sepsis. Happens every year.[6]

Here, Dr. Gamma outlines the full range of concerns as they relate to cancer and other immune-compromised patients writ large that was offered by other physicians in the study as well. All diseases carry the risk of severe complica-

---

6. This participant interview excerpt is also quoted in "When Patients Question Vaccines: Considering Vaccine Communication through a Material Rhetorical Approach," page 171.

tions, even for healthy children and adults. Even if one healthy individual is able to fight off a vaccine-preventable disease, there is no way to know what the immune status is of the people with whom that individual interacts, even in casual contact with strangers on a daily basis. Dr. Gamma cites vaccinations as a way to mitigate these many unknowns associated with disease.

Furthermore, many pediatric cancer patients cannot be vaccinated or will lose immunity once beginning treatment, so they rely on population-level immunity to protect them from contagion during and after treatment. Dr. Gamma described how this need to protect cancer patients often demands significant effort on the part of families of a child with cancer. For example, siblings who have not had chickenpox must be vaccinated so that they do not accidentally bring chickenpox home from school and infect their sibling undergoing treatment for cancer. However, they also cannot have any contact following vaccination, because varicella is a live-virus vaccine that actually can transmit attenuated varicella, which is a weakened form of chickenpox that can still be serious to the immune-compromised. As a result, siblings must often be vaccinated and then stay away from the family for a week or practice other safety measures to ensure the cancer patient is protected by a cocoon of immunity in the family. This need extends to the child's outside community as well:

> And in fact, one of the things that we tell families, you know, cause they'll say, "What can we do to help this family?" and I'll say, "Tell everybody to get the chickenpox vaccine at school so your child can go to school safely." Yeah, so, because, you know, if their classmate breaks out with chickenpox, it means, you know, a long stay in the hospital for them, it interrupts their therapy, it decreases the chances that we're gonna cure them. It's huge. . . huge. Same thing with the flu. So, you know, these diseases are devastating to the population I treat, and so I get very twitchy when people don't want to vaccinate.[7]

Here, Dr. Gamma articulates the stakes of community vaccination for cancer patients very clearly: not only does vaccination keep a child with cancer protected from vaccine-preventable diseases but vaccination helps ensure the efficacy of chemotherapy treatment, meaning a difference between life and death for a child undergoing intensive care. Preventing these conditions is a primary professional concern for doctors in these different practices, demonstrating

---

7. This participant interview excerpt is also quoted in "When Patients Question Vaccines: Considering Vaccine Communication through a Material Rhetorical Approach," page 171.

how the doctor's background and context of disease shapes the vaccines they require, the objects they use, and the rhetorics they employ to characterize the vaccine's importance to patients.

Local Contexts and Professional Practices

Professional issues relevant to local community contexts also factor in to doctor's perspectives on vaccination. In this locality, an outbreak of pertussis occurred in spring 2011 among children in a private school that was lax in its vaccination requirements in a nearby county. Even though none of the physicians I interviewed were directly involved in that incident, it nonetheless caused practices throughout the area to respond in a variety of ways, consequently changing these doctors' practices and policies.

Most significantly, in fall 2011, a private area pediatric practice, ABC Pediatrics, changed its vaccination policy to state that families who would not vaccinate according to AAP guidelines would no longer be seen by the practice. Families who were currently seen by ABC Pediatrics and were not up-to-date on vaccinations had to choose whether they would receive the required vaccinations or select another practice for their pediatric care. I interviewed two doctors from that practice, Drs. Zeta and Kappa, who both described the policy as a decision that was difficult to make. Although the original proposals for the policy had been initiated years earlier, ultimately the outbreak in a neighboring community tipped the scales in favor of such a policy. Both doctors cited the need to protect other children in the practice who had compromised immune systems in the event of another outbreak. Dr. Kappa, who described himself as one of the physicians who led the effort to institute the new policy, characterized the rationale for the policy as follows:

> You have 5% of the population that really relies on other people who are healthy and can get vaccinated to be vaccinated. There are the children who, maybe they have cancer, the others have a parent or a grandparent who has cancer, then you have someone who's had an organ transplant. We've got some kids who are walking around this office with heart transplants. They're on immuno-suppressive agents. They cannot be vaccinated . . . they just can't. So, their risk in their own waiting room was an issue. . . . And then we have another child over here whose family has decided to decline the vaccine and has come in with some symptoms that could be vaccine-preventable illness that's very contagious and could be deadly to the same child with the heart.

He also stated that nonvaccinating families posed risks to larger health care systems, including hospitals, since parents may take children with very high fevers or other ailments to the emergency room for treatment without alerting the hospital staff that the child is not fully vaccinated. This behavior posed, again, the risk of putting others with compromised immune systems in hospitals in jeopardy of catching highly contagious, vaccine-preventable diseases.

Dr. Delta, a general pediatrician not affiliated with this practice, stated that the policy change at ABC Pediatrics affected her practice as well by forcing the office to respond with its own policy regarding vaccination. Although they chose to continue seeing existing patients who were hesitant toward vaccinations, they did restrict new patients, particularly in the immediate aftermath of the change at ABC Pediatrics:

> I think that all of us feel that vaccinations are very important, right across the board, and we have said as a practice that we would not take new patients that were not planning to vaccinate at all. . . . What our practice has said, and we did this after [ABC Pediatrics] came out with their statement. We said, okay, what are we gonna do? And we said very quickly we would not take their [patients] that they were following that were not vaccinating. That we didn't feel comfortable and that we didn't want to be seen as sort of the practice where everybody came who didn't want to vaccinate. And we said that partially because we felt like we had a responsibility to our other patients. If we agreed to bring in all of those people that don't vaccinate, then sitting in the waiting room, we're putting our patients at risk.

At Dr. Beta's ob/gyn practice, the situation was also complicated by the simple logistics of shared office space with those who saw patients who became ill with pertussis during the outbreak. Dr. Beta recounts: "I had to go get pertussis booster because we share office space with the family practice from which that kid with whooping cough came. So, that and the kids at that school in [nearby county], a lot of those kids came to the family practice where I share office space. So I had to go . . . get my pertussis vaccination." Although he did not report that this had a significant impact on his practice, he also stated, "Now, there's also our recent, some recent emphasis on pertussis because they had a whooping cough outbreak in [nearby county]. And so, they kind of brought that back to the kind of forefront." Thus, smaller, local contexts of professional discourses and practices also influence doctors' needs for vaccine and the vaccine's ontology-in-practice, since the vaccine takes on a new operation in the context of an outbreak of infectious disease that puts an entire region in immediate risk. Ultimately, the consequences shift significantly for patients as well, who may be more likely to request (or be required to obtain) vaccinations.

DISEASES, CURES, AND PREVENTION: MATERIAL EXIGENCIES OF DISEASE IN VACCINATION DISCOURSE

Examining doctors' communication about vaccinations shows how current conceptions of vaccine controversy, understood as chiefly a problem created by misguided or mistaken parent beliefs, are incredibly limited. Vaccinations play an important role in medical practice and are reflective of a particular stance toward disease—one that emphasizes prevention rather than treatment or cure. Intervening in disease by preventing instead of managing or treating it means that the object of that intervention has a particular ontology-in-practice, shaping and shaped by the physician's professional stance, one that works primarily to avoid infectious disease. When examined from this perspective, three major factors emerge as significant ways to rethink why vaccines remain so controversial.

First, vaccines are professional objects that dictate how doctors do disease (Mol) by intervening via prevention, not cure. By responding to disease primarily through prevention, doctors are able to distance their practice from the things that disease signifies, such as severe symptoms, inadequate treatments, unsafe waiting rooms, and the responsibility of a gravely ill patient. The tension between doing disease through prevention instead of through cure becomes clearest in the discourses about meningitis and the vaccines that prevent it (Hib, PCV, and MCV), which is perhaps why it was mentioned by doctors so frequently in the interviews. Doctors describe meningitis as severe, life-threatening, and quick-moving—the kind of disease where the doctor's only way of responding is inadequate (pushing antibiotics in the right dosage to kill the disease but not the patient) and invasive (spinal taps and blood tests on an already gravely ill child). And even if those attempts were successful, children could still end up with life-altering conditions or disfigurement. In this case, the ways doctors do meningitis are largely uncertain and full of failure. By contrast, a vaccinated child who presents with a high fever will not be suspected of being infected with Hib, pneumococcal, or meningococcal diseases. Spinal taps will not be necessary. High doses of broad-spectrum antibiotics will wait. Consequently, the vaccination is a way of doing something different—it is an intervention in disease that produces health not through cure, but through prevention.

Vaccinations also configure disease exigence with equipment for management and control, as they affect both an individual patient and others in the community. In this sense, preventing disease renders the disease both smaller and larger than the patient, as seen from the view of the doctor. Diseases are small, microbial agents that the doctor can prevent at the microscopic level within the body through the vaccination. That smallness also facilitates their opportunistic movement among the healthy and the sick. Yet if disease is not prevented, it becomes bigger, engaging entire systems and networks of resources if even one patient becomes ill. And disease becomes bigger still when it spreads beyond the individual and infects other, more vulnerable members of a practice who put themselves at risk simply by sitting in the doctor's waiting room. Vaccines become the linchpin in the entire apparatus of prevention by controlling disease at the micro level in a patient, ensuring safety at the macro level as well.

The issue of waiting room safety and immune-compromised patients also factored significantly into the doctors' rationales for supporting vaccines, again correlating the need for the vaccine to disease. Doctors, by the very nature of their jobs, see a wide range of illnesses that the average person who does not work in the health care industry is unlikely to see. Diseases are described as having their own agency as they move through a community and pass from "healthy" people who can fight them off to those who cannot. As Dr. Gamma states, chickenpox might be fine for a healthy child, but the risk is that the child will pass varicella to a person with cancer, a recent transplant patient, or an elderly person with a weakened immune system.

By contrast, most people outside of the health care industry can go days, weeks, or even lifetimes without encountering people who they know are sick with serious, chronic conditions that affect the immune system. This stance further reinforces Mol's idea of multiple, coexisting realities in medical practice—when a doctor examines a patient sick with chickenpox, that doctor does not just treat that child and that case of chickenpox. Other factors are implicated in that case of chickenpox: another child with a heart transplant, unable to fight even a minor childhood disease because of immuno-suppressive medication; an immune-compromised grandparent who might have cared for the child for the afternoon before the child was symptomatic; and a contaminated waiting room. Meanwhile, the child sick with chickenpox is something entirely different to the parent—a week of lost work, a household of children who may become ill, a potential trip to the emergency room in the case of complications, and so forth. Responding to disease exigence, for doctors, does not just involve the immediate patient but is an interaction that happens between the doctor and the disease itself, as the doctor becomes responsible not just for treating the person but also for controlling the damage the disease can do beyond a single patient.

This desire to contain and manage diseases via prevention may also further complicate the highly publicized, though scientifically debunked, association between vaccinations and autism. The doctors interviewed often reported that MMR was the vaccine most parents were worried about and asked the most questions about. Yet none of the doctors interviewed stated that measles, mumps, or rubella were among the diseases they were most concerned about their patients contracting. These diseases were rarely even mentioned, particularly in comparison to meningitis or chickenpox. From the perspective of doctors, in some ways, the vaccine–autism controversy amplifies the frustrations they have with vaccine skepticism when it comes to the ways they do disease. Not only did the specious connections posted between autism and MMR call into question the MMR vaccination, meaning that doctors were forced to reassure parents that the vaccine is, from their perspective, completely safe, but through challenges to the safety of vaccine ingredients—preservatives, adjuvants, and other components of all vaccinations—all vaccines became suspect for some parents. As a result, the fears about a vaccine that protects against less consequential diseases put children at increased risk for diseases for which the doctor's most effective method of intervention is prevention.

 Second, the vaccine's materiality also greatly influences doctors' practices. As material objects, vaccines carry with them a range of professional issues beyond the risks and benefits of vaccines versus the diseases they prevent. Although vaccinations can be administered in a variety of places, including pharmacies, schools, the local health department, and even Walmart, vaccines compose a significant portion of what many doctors, particularly pediatricians, do. Vaccines must be ordered, properly stored, and maintained in quantities that are appropriate to practice administration to ensure that vaccines are neither scarce nor unused. Vaccinations are administered mostly through highly specialized means and procedures—not just anyone can perform a vaccination. Vaccines, particularly pneumococcal vaccine, undergo frequent updates to protect against more and more strains of the disease, meaning that vaccine records must be carefully monitored to ensure that the most appropriate vaccination is given at any time. Furthermore, some manufacturers create combined vaccinations from vaccines typically given at the same time and are trademarked under different brand names (such as Pediarix, developed by GlaxoSmithKline, which combines the DTaP, hepatitis B, and polio vaccines). So if vaccinations are given at multiple doctors' offices, or if different vaccinations are available depending on the circumstances at an appointment, doctors and nurses must be careful to not duplicate vaccinations or deliver a vaccination at the incorrect time. From the large, significant consequences that might come from a contaminated waiting room to the minutiae of paperwork and storage processes, vaccines take up significant amounts of space and energy in doctors' offices to ensure they are available to be administered properly.

Finally, understanding vaccine controversy as discord motivated by competing, yet unresolved, material exigencies offers a useful rhetorical paradigm for demonstrating why the issue defies easy discursive response. For physicians and patients (and parents of patients), vaccines are different objects to them simultaneously. Ignoring the separate, yet coexistent, exigencies to which doctors and patients respond has allowed the materiality of the vaccination to be obscured by the discourses that emerge around it—those about autism and reactions and allergies and myths that people read on the internet and even doctors' insistence that parents "get the facts." What might appear to be arguments that engage the ethos of the doctor versus the parent, the logos of scientific fact, or the pathos of a mother's emotional reaction to a story she read on the internet, when examined through a material rhetorical approach, reveal an entirely different phenomenon. Vaccines are objects of intervention that are essential to the profession's critical mission to prevent, rather than cure, disease. For doctors, it is not that vaccines are simply time-tested, or very effective, or scientifically proven to be safe that makes them so important; it is that vaccination facilitates a way of responding to disease that intervenes and produces the certainty of prevention rather than the uncertainties of disease. Yet this is the point at which parents and doctors might differ most significantly. Where the doctor administers medicine that avoids meningitis, parents obtain a shot, a medication given to a perfectly healthy child with the purpose of making it sick, even if it is in a small, scarcely detectable way. These are differences in the realities of doctors and parents that must be accounted for and addressed if this public controversy is to be understood as anything other than a power- and expertise-based binary between expert and lay sources of knowledge.

CHANGING DISEASE: TOWARD INTERVENTION AND ERADICATION

These findings offer an explanation for discord that produces and facilitates vaccination controversy not produced by parental deficit but rather complicated by a wide range of material exigencies that remain unaddressed across the practice of vaccination. Such an alternate view offers important lessons for those hoping to intervene in vaccination controversy—and for RHM scholars in particular—in widening the scope of understanding of how vaccines shape and change discourse. Once available, vaccination gives a disease the status of being "vaccine-preventable," which then makes the vaccine-preventable disease an unnecessary risk for individuals and communities (discussed further as material exigencies of eradication in chapter 2). As these analyses show, the benefits of vaccination to physicians are expressed in value-laden terms directly linked to and shaped by disease exigencies and professional constraints. As material exigence, the value of vaccination stretches far beyond just the prevention of disease in individuals. Vaccination is an instrumental means through which disease exigence is addressed—by preventing quick-moving, severe disease; reducing the need to perform invasive, uncertain diagnostic procedures; and avoiding the unnecessary use of treatments that carry high-risk side effects. Such an understanding of how vaccines create material exigencies helps to offer rhetorical explanations for discord.

A goal of protecting community members, and particularly vulnerable ones, from disease initiates correlative material exigencies, primarily enacted through public health policy. As seen here, the objectives of individual and community protection are closely interrelated possibilities created by vaccination. But as rates of infection and cases of diseases slowly trickle down to zero, a disease-free future wherein the deadliest communicable diseases are eradicated entirely seems like an achievable goal on a nearby horizon. Inspired by the successes of smallpox, the first vaccine to be completely eradicated by a vaccine, eradicating diseases like measles, polio, and flu remains a goal of scientific research, medical practice, and public health policy, constituting and shaping another material exigence in vaccine controversy—that of eradication.

CHAPTER 2

Community Immunity and the Promise of Eradication

IN DECEMBER 2014 the happiest place on earth turned into a hotbed for infectious disease, specifically, measles—an extremely contagious, deadly illness. In mid-December, someone infected with the measles virus visited Disneyland in Anaheim, California, and inadvertently infected dozens of other visitors there. (This "patient zero" was never identified.) In the ensuing weeks, this initial measles exposure at Disneyland turned into an international epidemic, eventually sickening people in eight states and across international lines. Young babies were quarantined. Adults with waning immunity were at risk. Children with compromised immune systems innocently sitting in their pediatrician's waiting rooms were endangered.

Circulated swiftly and surely, media reports about the outbreak asserted who was at fault for this devastation: the antivaccination movement. Emboldened by faux facts propagated by former Playboy bunnies, fraudulent doctors, and pseudoscience, antivaccinationists had finally reached such a critical mass that they had done irrevocable damage to herd immunity, reducing it to such a low state that deadly diseases could return and spread. These vaccination truants, these herd-immunity free-riders, these *idiots*—they were at fault, and they needed to be stopped.

In addition to general blame placed on "the antivaccination movement," specific blame was focused on California's personal belief exemption (PBE) to vaccinations. PBEs required only that a parent declare a "personal belief" in opposition to vaccination in order to avoid one or all vaccines. PBEs had long been available to residents of California, but increased rates of PBEs and associated low rates of vaccination were, according to provaccine politicians and policymakers, jeopardizing herd immunity at the local level, particularly in wealthier, primarily white parts of Southern California where the outbreak initially took hold (Majumder; Atwell et al.; Bowes). The Disneyland outbreak was a step too far. Ultimately, outrage over the outbreak was transformed into political action, culminating in the change of California law to remove all but medically documented vaccine exemptions.

Such a case is a prime example of the material exigencies of vaccinations at work—and in the case of public health, the exigency of disease *eradication,* the material exigence examined in this chapter. As chapter 1 discusses, material exigencies of disease shape and constrain discourses about vaccination as they impact professional practice, the daily work of doctors, and the nature of infectious disease. This chapter extends that analysis further, demonstrating how the vaccine's power to eradicate disease makes eradication a powerful material exigence, demanding response, constraining discourse, and fueling discord across the issue. The theory of community, or herd, immunity holds that once a certain number of members of a community are immune to disease, the disease will no longer spread, protecting the more vulnerable members of the herd from infection. Technically, this immunity can be developed through actually acquiring a disease or through the immune protection of vaccination, the latter being preferable since it carries fewer risks and less overall impact on health systems (Fine et al.).[1] Eradication functions as a step beyond mere population protection, however, requiring significant, multinational efforts and mass population buy-in (or, in the absence of that, significant regulatory power to mandate vaccines) and has vanquishing a disease as its end, not just stopping or mitigating outbreaks. Forcing every person on the globe to acquire a disease in order to eventually stop its spread is too time-consuming, resource-intensive, and ethically specious to actually execute, of

---

1. Herd immunity, as Paul Fine, Ken Eames, and David Heymann describe, refers to a set of concepts regarding populations and protection from disease:

> Some authors use [herd immunity] to describe the proportion immune among individuals in a population. Others use it with reference to a particular threshold proportion of immune individuals that should lead to a decline in incidence of infection. Still others use it to refer to a pattern of immunity that should protect a population from invasion of a new infection. A common implication of the term is that the risk of infection among susceptible individuals in a population is reduced by the presence and proximity of immune individuals (this is sometimes referred to as "indirect protection" or a "herd effect"). (911)

course—but it is within the power of public health to administer vaccines into mouths, arms, or noses worldwide under the edict of eradication.

In this chapter, the argumentation in the course of the Disneyland public health crisis and ensuing policy change is examined as an example of the ways in which discourse is constrained by material exigencies of eradication. This chapter begins by charting the history of eradication as it relates to vaccination and public health policy and how public health policy in the US is articulated and enacted as a series of medico-legal rhetorics.[2] Medico-legal rhetorics, as conceptualized here, are arguments in the space between medicine, science, and the law where they work together to regulate, define, and reify normative ways for constructing and legislating bodies, what they do, how they behave, and how they respond to interventions (Lawrence "Medicolegal Rhetorics"; Grant et al.). Through an analysis of media reports in response to the 2014 measles outbreak, I examine how the media used existing concerns about California's exemption laws, constructions of measles as a "once-eliminated" scourge, and reification of public perceptions about those who choose not to vaccinate to shift exemption policy and argue for measles eradication. Overall, this analysis examines the role of eradication as material exigence—how this material need creates limits on what diseases are permitted to do within communities, what discourses can be used and what they can do, and how public health policies about vaccines gain power.

MATERIAL EXIGENCE: MEDICO-LEGAL RHETORICS AND SMALLPOX ERADICATION

The term *medico-legal* has a long history in the fields of medicine and law, where it defines the ways in which the two professions intersect. A search for the term *medico-legal* in the *Journal of the American Medical Association* reveals a lengthy evolution of this term and how it has worked for medical and law professionals, dating to 1885.[3] The law looks to medicine to provide court

---

2. The notion of medico-legal rhetorics was also developed by my colleagues Amy Reed and Lenny Grant and me for our 2016 RSA panel, previously cited in text here. I want to give them additional credit here for the development and connection of this idea to my own work. Our conversations and conceptualizations of how medico-legal rhetorics worked were informative to how I understood the operations of rhetorics as expressed in this chapter. I am in their debt for the time and conversations that allowed me to make the arguments expressed here.

3. Articles through the late nineteenth and early twentieth centuries reporting on medico-legal events in *JAMA* describe the historical role that medicine and law played together in establishing (1) the role that X-rays could play as evidence in injury cases; (2) what liabilities employers had when employees "met with accidents" while working; (3) the first breathalyzer

cases with scientific definitions and boundaries, for ways to prove the disease or health patterns of an individual or community, and for ways to determine culpability in cases of injury. Medicine looks to the law for various forms of reification as well, most notably in malpractice suits, but also in adjudicating medical licenses (an important issue during medicine's early moves to professionalize in the nineteenth century), determining individual rights to privacy and personal liberty in the cases of contagious disease, and outlining the proper protocols for medical decisions made on behalf of minors or people who cannot make decisions for themselves.

For rhetoricians, medico-legal rhetorics do not apply just to distinct discourses where, literally, medical and legal experts converge to testify about DNA or blood spatter or medical negligence. Rather, medico-legal rhetorics function as a larger set of discourses where medicine and the law work together to decide larger questions about who is sick and who is healthy; what sickness and health are and are not; what the rights are of the healthy and the sick; who is responsible for ensuring health and mitigating sickness; and what should be done for those who are sick and by whom. Here, I am building upon the notion of medico-legal collaboration as conceptualized by Mary Lay Schuster, Brian Larson, and Amy Propen.[4] As Schuster, Larson, and Propen conceptualize it, medico-legal collaboration works rhetorically to co-constitute medical diagnoses and conditions with appropriate legal ramifications, wherein the discourses of each discipline begin to converge and co-constitute pathology and consequence. By separating out, in the case of sex offenders, "normal" and "other" citizens, the medico-legal space is not merely a discursive one but a site of material collaboration between powerful actors (91–92). Consequently, medico-legal rhetorics work to take constellations of discourses and stabilize them by scientizing, defining, and legislating the mechanisms of the body into routine, normative expectations against which abnormal bodies, reactions, and behaviors can be stigmatized.

Medico-legal rhetorics operate in vaccination through the policies that have developed, primarily over the course of the twentieth century in the US, to embed the public health objective to eradicate disease into law. Such

---

technology, where doctors worked to establish the relationship between levels of intoxication and alcohol detection on the breath; and (4) the legal definitions of conditions like alcoholism, "imbecility," and proper grounds for institutionalization in cases of insanity.

4. The notion of medico-legal rhetorics was also developed by my colleagues Amy Reed, Lenny Grant, and me for our 2016 RSA panel, previously cited in text here. I want to give them additional credit here for the development and connection of this idea to my own work. Our conversations and conceptualizations of how medico-legal rhetorics worked were informative to how I understood the operations of rhetorics as expressed in this chapter. I am in their debt for the time and conversations that allowed me to make the arguments expressed here.

a transformation empowered public health to have incredible influence over disease, medicine, and science during the twentieth century and continuing today, using medico-legal rhetorics to respond to eradication as a material exigence. Medico-legal rhetorics fix discourses to place, space, and time—laws and policies have particular jurisdictions, boundaries, and definitions for the people to whom they apply and the terms under which they are applicable. So, analyzing and examining medico-legal rhetorics can help us see, specifi- cally, where a term, concept, or problem becomes stabilized—or attempts to become stabilized—for a particular group and at a particular time. We can also then trace that stabilization moving forward into future iterations, appli- cations, documents, and revisions of those laws and policies. Because med- ico-legal rhetorics solidify and concretize formless or transient experiences and conditions through the repeated interactions of medicine and the law, another main tenet of medico-legal rhetoric is its end goal of stripping situ- ations of their rhetoricity. Medical discourses, through their appeals to and uses of science, aim to make human experiences observable and quantifiable. Corresponding laws and policies codify these observable, quantifiable traits into regulations, infractions, and punishments. Ultimately, therefore, medico-legal rhetorics create arhetorical situations out of rhetorical ones by making them into situations that can no longer be modified by discourse. Once the regulation has been broken, only regulatory action often remains. Through medico-legal rhetoric, the possibilities of eradication as a material exigence can be realized through laws and attendant discourses that demand response (and usually, compliance).

Smallpox and the Promise of Eradication

The history of vaccination policy is tied to the history of smallpox, the only disease to have been globally eradicated by a vaccine. Smallpox has had a long history that has shaped and been shaped by how humans have inter- acted, moved, and populated the world. It is an old virus, dating at least to 4 AD, though it is possible that it is older. Over the course of many centuries, it spread across Asia, through the Middle East, and to Europe and Africa. Colonization brought it to North and South America, where it caused mass infections and fatalities among indigenous populations. The variola virus itself makes particularly good use of the constructs and constraints of urban cen- ters: it is only transmitted among humans, it spreads easily from person to person through the air or on contaminated materials, and it either kills or confers long-term immunity on its host after a finite infectious phase. These characteristics ensured that epidemics could start easily in places where people were concentrated. Although there are many strains of orthopoxviruses that create related diseases in other species (such as cowpox, which infects cows but also people), only variola spreads from human to human without the need for contact with animals, making city centers optimal breeding grounds for the disease. Conferral of nearly lifelong immunity (for those who survived) would also produce a population of caregivers who could care for the newly sick relatively risk free (Durbach; Walloch; Kitta; Willrich).

The long-term immunity that infection produced ultimately made smallpox a good candidate for prevention, first through a process called variolation, and then through vaccination, leading to the eventual eradication of the disease. Not all infectious diseases produce such forms of immunity; herpes viruses recur, diseases like syphilis do not offer lifelong immunity after they are contracted, and flu viruses notoriously mutate so much that every flu season brings new risks for even the previously ill, to name just a few examples (CDC, "Syphilis"). Smallpox infection also carried readily available material for experimentation in the pustules that erupted on the bodies of the infected, giving people access to a form of the virus without the need for the materials, lab equipment, or even germ theory necessary to create immunity-inducing therapies. Prevention of smallpox through variolation is reported as early as 590 AD in China and was eventually brought to Europe by Lady Mary Wortley Montagu in 1718. Variolation exposed healthy people to the variola virus with material from the pustules of a person infected with active smallpox; small abrasions were made on the arm or another part of a healthy person's body, and the extracted material was applied to the abrasions (dried material from crusts of pustules could also be inhaled). The resulting infection produced a mild form of disease that made the recipient immune to smallpox. The immunity resulting from variolation was not as long-lasting as it often was from a full infection, but the process was effective enough to make it common practice throughout Europe and its colonies through the eighteenth century (Kitta 8–9). In England in the late eighteenth century, using similar principles but a different process, Dr. Edward Jenner developed the practice of vaccination, which soon became the preferred method of response to smallpox (Allen 49; Jenner).[5] Although vaccination was often a crude, imprecise, and ineffective procedure that included risks like secondary infections and illnesses (such as sepsis and tetanus) and severe scarring and permanent injury,

---

5. Jenner hypothesized that cowpox, a related infection but one that, as the name suggests, primarily infected cows, might be protective against the far more serious smallpox.

these instances were perceived to be neither as frequent nor as severe as with variolation (Walloch 11–20).

PREVENTION AND THE PUBLIC GOOD: TOWARD COMMUNITY IMMUNITY

Although the actual application of the theory of herd immunity to vaccine-preventable disease did not happen until the 1970s (Fine et al.), the idea of vaccinating an individual to protect others in the community predated this notion. Specifically, vaccinating for the benefit of the community, and valuing those needs over those of the individual, set the medico-legal stage for the 1905 Supreme Court ruling *Jacobson v. Massachusetts*, which would create the national legal precedent to compel vaccination in the US. Prior to *Jacobson*, those fighting mass vaccination orders used a variety of arguments to oppose such arguments, such as safety concerns about the vaccination materials, individual health risks associated with the vaccine, and the necessity and ethics of vaccination orders (Walloch).[6] Henning Jacobson, the complainant in the case, was not an active antivaccinationist, though his case was eventually taken up by the Massachusetts Antivaccination Society, which was active and robust at that time.[7] Jacobson had been vaccinated before and, he felt, had experienced reactions to the vaccine so severe that he felt he should not have to subject himself to the vaccination again. In 1900 a smallpox outbreak

---

6. Historical studies about vaccination concern and scientific publications about vaccinations published in the late nineteenth and early twentieth centuries—particularly the work of Karen Walloch—have demonstrated that these concerns were once quite real, commonplace, and verifiable. Before regulations like the Pure Food and Drug Act of 1902 were brought to bear on vaccinations, these materials were often made by companies without consistent practice or control. It was not unheard of for the vaccinated to contract disease from the vaccine itself, develop life-threatening sepsis from staph infections caused by the vaccination materials, contract diseases like hepatitis or tetanus from improperly purified vaccinations, or simply receive products that were sold as vaccinations that actually did nothing at all.

7. From the first vaccinations there were vocal opponents to the practice, organized in a range of antivaccination societies and leagues across many states. Opposition to smallpox vaccination in the US in the nineteenth century was shaped by a few specific characteristics that continue to impact vaccination controversy in the US today: the organization and implementation of vaccination mandates by local authorities, experience with the disease itself, and varying medical perspectives and opinions on vaccination. Antivaccination sentiments and groups tended to be decentralized in nineteenth-century America; these groups also organized in response to local ordinances and vaccination mandates. Therefore, opposition became highly localized, even levied in response to specific local health officials with whom people had existing conflicts. Varying forms of variola virus contributed to local opposition to smallpox vaccine as well (Willrich).

in Cambridge, Massachusetts, where Jacobson and his family lived, prompted city officials to impose a vaccination mandate. Vaccinators from the department of public health went door-to-door and offered vaccinations for free; anyone who didn't agree to be vaccinated would be charged a $5 fine—at a time when average wages were $13/week—and possible jail time (Willrich 374). Michael Willrich recounts:

> But young Henning's vaccination had gone badly. He experienced "great and extreme suffering" that instilled in him a lifelong horror of the practice. . . . One of Jacobson's boys (he did not say which) suffered adverse effects from a childhood vaccination, convincing the minister that some hereditary condition in his family made vaccine a particular hazard for them. Jacobson's belief that smallpox vaccine threatened his family's existence seemed as deeply ingrained as his religious faith. (377)

At the time, exemptions to vaccine mandates were only available for children, and Jacobson argued that this same protection should be available to adults. This refusal was made during the tenure of a particularly zealous health commissioner in Cambridge, who battled antivaccinationism and felt that strict enforcement of vaccination mandates was absolutely essential to a proper response to disease (Walloch). Massachusetts health commissioners countered that an individual's discomfort or risk from the vaccine was not a sufficient rationale to risk jeopardizing the health of the entire community—to further complicate this, shopkeepers, hoteliers, and other merchants added concern about the potential damage to businesses if smallpox were to break out and sick people stayed home and healthy people avoided townships and gathering spaces for fear of getting sick (Walloch).

Jacobson was charged the fine by the Commonwealth of Massachusetts but appealed the penalty, eventually reaching the Supreme Court, where he appealed the power of the public health authority over the individual protections afforded by the Fourteenth Amendment. However, the decision was not made in his favor; the court eventually ruled 7–2 to protect the right of the state to compel individuals to vaccinate in the face of crisis to public safety, and a smallpox outbreak qualified as such a crisis. The following is from the majority opinion of the *Jacobson v. Massachusetts* ruling:

> Eleven [of his objections to vaccination] all relate to alleged injurious or dangerous effects of vaccination. The defendant "offered to prove and show by competent evidence" these so-called facts. Each of them, in its nature,

is such that it cannot be stated as a truth, otherwise than as a matter of opinion. . . .

Assuming that medical experts could have been found who would have testified in support of these propositions . . . [the judge] would have considered this testimony of experts in connection with the facts, that for nearly a century, most of the members of the medical profession have regarded vaccination, repeated after intervals, as a preventive of smallpox.

While [experts] have recognized the possibility of injury to an individual from carelessness in the performance of it, or even, in a conceivable case, without carelessness, they generally have considered the risk of such an injury too small to be seriously weighed as against the benefits coming from the discreet and proper use of the preventive. (Harlan, *Henning Jacobson v. Commonwealth of Massachusetts*)

The precedents set by the language in this ruling use medico-legal rhetorics to stabilize important definitions, concepts, and experiences relevant in this case to vaccination.[8] In this case, the ruling establishes what counts as facts (the testimony of medical experts over the anecdotal experiences of lay individuals), what counts as truth within those contexts, and what types of claims and injuries to individuals are reasonable when balanced against community good. Hence, not only does the *Jacobson* case set the legal precedence that allows communities to mandate vaccines; it does so using medico-legal rhetorical practices to make the situation surrounding vaccine refusal arhetorical, putting the community good over the individual and compelling an individual to comply with vaccine regulations.

Compelling Eradication

Although vaccination's power to eradicate the centuries-old plague of smallpox is often noted among vaccination's successes, the actual means through which that eradication happened are less often noted alongside this narrative. By the 1950s smallpox had declined internationally and remained endemic in only a few places in the world, namely parts of Africa and Asia. At the same

---

8. Significantly, and ominously, *Jacobson v. Massachusetts* was cited as precedent by Oliver Wendell Holmes in *Buck v. Bell,* in which the Supreme Court allowed the forced sterilization of "imbeciles." In his majority opinion, Holmes states: "The principle that sustains compulsory vaccination is broad enough to cover cutting the Fallopian tubes. Three generations of imbeciles are enough," and specifically cites the Jacobson ruling (*Buck v. Bell*).

time, the vaccine continued to be administered to children in the US and Europe, despite the fact that cases of smallpox were exceedingly rare (Colgrove, *State of Immunity*). Worldwide eradication of smallpox was first discussed by the (then new) World Health Organization (WHO) in the 1950s, and the actual campaign to eradicate the disease began in the early 1960s (Bhattacharya). Over the course of a decade, WHO organized its regional health offices and local contacts to coordinate mass vaccination programs throughout Asia, Africa, and South America to, essentially, achieve international herd immunity through vaccination (Bhattacharya). Note that this goal of eradication was achieved not through grassroots efforts, local coordinated vaccination campaigns, or a demand by nations where smallpox was endemic. Rather, a top-down regulatory mandate largely composed of experts in developed nations required vaccination of those living in developing ones. Although WHO strategy and goals were informed and implemented through the cooperation of local health officials and providers in areas where campaigns were run, ultimately the political imperatives, practices, and initiatives for global eradication came from outside local communities.

Global smallpox eradication benefited not only the areas where smallpox was endemic but also the countries that no longer experienced smallpox, because vaccination (with its attendant risks) was able to be phased out. By midcentury, smallpox was no longer a significant threat to public health in the US; other childhood diseases, like measles and polio, and chronic conditions, like heart disease, posed increasingly bigger risks (Colgrove, "Immunity for the People" 251). However, smallpox vaccine was still routinely administered amid fears that travelers from places where smallpox was still endemic would be able to create an epidemic in the US. As the worldwide eradication efforts began to experience more success, however, the risks of continuing to vaccinate against smallpox loomed larger in comparison. As James Colgrove reports, "In 1966, researchers from the Public Health Service, in the first systematic attempt to document the scope of the problem in the United States, determined that out of an estimated fourteen million smallpox vaccinations administered in a single year, there were more than four hundred severe reactions and seven deaths" (163). By 1971 the Advisory Committee on Immunization Practices (ACIP) officially changed its recommendation on smallpox vaccine (Colgrove 166).

Therefore, the (usually celebratory) trope that smallpox was eradicated from the planet through vaccination should be understood as more complex than is often hailed in the grand narrative of vaccination. Yes, vaccination helped expunge a horrible scourge from the planet, which ultimately saved untold lives across the globe. However, that effort created significant forms of dissent, happened despite very serious risks and over a century of highly imprecise practices experienced by everyone who endured the procedure, and was ultimately achieved through a top-down coordinated international edict that mandated eradication. Such an effort is highly dependent upon very particular geopolitical climates, international mechanisms for cooperation, and scientific consensus that are hard to replicate in even the friendliest of environments for vaccines.

Perhaps most significantly for American vaccination policy, however, smallpox eradication created the hope of eradication as a goal for vaccine policy. As Colgrove and Elena Conis both argue, the possibilities of eradication established through smallpox vaccination would inevitably inform and shape the vaccine policies and mandates created in the 1960s and 1970s for universal vaccination for polio, measles, mumps, and rubella, though the goal of eradicating those diseases has yet to be achieved. This notion—that because vaccination *can* eradicate disease we therefore *should* eradicate it—has been uncritically accepted and has shaped vaccine policies in ways that continue to contribute to the contentious nature of vaccine discussions in doctors' offices and other public spaces today (Conis 7). The following discussion of vaccine mandates reflects the importance of eradication that we enact, primarily through the systematic vaccination of children and the use of school entry mandates to enforce and achieve this goal.

Eradication and Contemporary Health Policy

In the US today, vaccine mandates are primarily compelled through school and daycare entry, entry into colleges and universities, and requirements levied in some professions (primarily those in or related to the health care industry). Yet the regulatory apparatus surrounding vaccination is far more complex than simple school vaccination forms. The bodies that determine what vaccines are recommended and when they should be administered include federal bodies and professional organizations, such as the American Academy of Pediatrics (AAP), the American Academy of Family Physicians (AAFP), and the Centers for Disease Control and Prevention (CDC). These organizations also work together with private companies to identify vaccine needs and develop new vaccinations; work alongside the US Food and Drug Administration (FDA) to approve and license vaccines; and work with other governmental organizations (such as the National Institutes of Health [NIH] and WHO) to monitor diseases and assess vaccine efficacy. Although these organizations are incredibly powerful national voices in the vaccine debate and determine national directions for vaccine programs, funding for vaccine research and development, and, through their recommendations, what vaccines will be covered by insurance and other cost-saving programs, they are actually the least empowered to compel vaccination decisions. Outside of health emergencies, there are no federal laws requiring individual citizens to comply with CDC recommendations, and state-level requirements for vaccines for school entry can vary greatly from what the CDC recommends.

Consequently, vaccine mandates are enacted and enforced by a range of federal, state, local, and private regulations and controls. Recommended vaccinations begin shortly after birth and are administered throughout infancy, childhood, and into adulthood, meaning that what vaccines individuals get are partially determined by the stringency of the vaccine requirements in the hospital they are born in, the doctors they see, the school system they attend, and the professions they choose. Vaccines are mandated and controlled by states, and each state has different programs and practices available for enforcing their laws, uses different measures to ensure compliance, and even has different basic requirements for school and daycare entry. In most states, policymakers in the state legislature determine actual vaccine requirements for school entry, using official guidelines but not required to adopt them, and also deliberate over and determine the number of doses of vaccine that are acceptable for school entry and the types of exemptions—and the requirements for those exemptions—that the state will allow. As just one example of how stark the differences can be, Table 2 compares official CDC recommendations with state requirements in Virginia.

These recommendations differ primarily in rhetorical situation. CDC recommendations are meant to cover a young lifespan from birth to age five or six, but state-level regulations just determine what protections an individual must have in order to enter school; if a child avoids a school environment prior to age five or six, then in Virginia, that child can avoid Rotavirus vaccine, many doses of flu vaccine, as well as Hib and PCV vaccines, yet still be fully compliant with the law. In addition, there are few mechanisms other than school to ensure that an individual is vaccinated against MMR, DTaP, or hepatitis B on time. In the interim, individual doctors are the primary gatekeepers of CDC-recommended schedules, making doctors' offices the primary space where recommendations for things like Hib or pneumococcal disease are enacted.

Overall, the scope of vaccine requirements and laws is incredibly large, spanning governmental and professional requirements and recommendations (which carry virtually no legal power but incredible professional and persuasive influence) that are, ultimately, up to local school districts and indi-

TABLE 2. Vaccination requirements: CDC-recommended schedule compared with Virginia requirements for school and daycare entry

CDC (Recommended by the age of 6 as outlined in the 2018 requirements)	VIRGINIA (Minimum required for public school or daycare entry as of 2019)
3 doses of Hepatitis B	3 doses of Hepatitis B
2–3 doses of Rotavirus (depending on brand and timing)	Rotavirus: NOT REQUIRED
5 doses of DTaP	4 doses of DTaP
3–4 doses of Hib (depending on brand and timing)	1–3 doses of Hib (depending on brand and timing) only required up to 60 months of age
4 doses of PCV 13 (protects against pneumococcal infection)	1–4 doses of PCV 13 (protects against pneumococcal infection) (number of doses depends on brand and timing) only required up to 60 months of age
4 doses of polio vaccine	4 doses of polio vaccine
2 doses of flu vaccine after 6 months and annually thereafter for a possible total of 6 doses	Flu: NOT REQUIRED
2 doses of MMR	2 measles, 2 mumps, 1 rubella (though most children receive 2 doses of all since these vaccines are not available in separate doses, but still the official requirement is only 1 dose of rubella)
2 doses of varicella	2 doses of varicella or proof of immunity
2 doses of Hepatitis A	Hepatitis A: NOT REQUIRED
Total: If a parent follows the 2018 CDC-recommended schedule, by the age of 6, the child will have received up to 35 doses of vaccine.	Total: If a parent follows Virginia law in 2019, to enter kindergarten, a child will have received up to 22 doses of vaccine, including no vaccines against Rotavirus or flu and only vaccines against pneumococcal infection or Hib if a child went to a childcare facility before the age of 5.
(https://www.cdc.gov/vaccines/schedules/downloads/child/0-18yrs-child-combined-schedule.pdf)	(http://www.vdh.virginia.gov/immunization/requirements/)

vidual medical providers to enforce. As a result, parents experience highly local constraints on and consequences for their choices in their communities as they navigate the expectations of medical, governmental, and even religious authorities. In this sense, local community values dictate which vaccines parents get for their children more than the CDC does.

These overlapping regulatory bodies and influences add complexity to experiences of and requirements for vaccination across the US as well as our understanding of the depth, breadth, and scope of vaccine controversy, particularly at the state level. Wang et al.'s 2014 review of nonmedical exemptions across the US found great variability in the types of exemptions filed, the vaccination rates among those who had received exemptions (some reported being partially to nearly fully vaccinated and were just missing some vaccines or boosters), and the reported reasons for the exemption. For example, Wang et al. find that in states with PBEs, parents had filed exemptions when faced with incomplete vaccine records or other logistical impediments just to avoid having titers taken or children revaccinated if the quantity of boosters was in question. Furthermore, there is a significant disconnect between when most vaccines are delivered—between birth and age five—and the actual mechanisms for tracking and holding parents accountable to vaccine requirements, which may happen as late as kindergarten entry. Therefore, a child easily can remain unvaccinated throughout infancy and toddlerhood and just catch up on vaccines prior to school entry. Such a child would present a risk to community health but may not be recorded as a vaccine refuser through exemptions since those might not be needed until much later in a child's life. Yet mandates—and exemptions to those mandates—are a key site of discord in vaccine controversy because they mediate political intervention into and control over vaccination practices.

EXEMPTIONS, ERADICATION, AND THE DISNEYLAND MEASLES EPIDEMIC

Disneyland is in Anaheim, in Southern California. Much of this part of the country is wealthy, highly educated, and white—all factors that are perceived to be part of the problem when it comes to vaccine refusal. At the time of the outbreak, California had three options for vaccine exemptions, which together made an exemption easier to obtain in California than in other states. Although all states offer medical exemptions for vaccinations, forty-eight offer religious exemptions, and only nineteen offer exemptions for philosophical or personal belief, or those based on personal belief only. California offered all three kinds of exemptions at the time of the outbreak, a policy that dated to the 1960s (Gold). So, prior to the policy change, in California, in order for a child or adult to avoid any mandatory vaccination, that person simply must register a philosophical exemption to vaccination, and the person can avoid all vaccines, avoid only some, or negotiate a modified schedule with a practitioner.

Beginning in the late 1990s, however, in light of controversies surrounding the since-retracted Wakefield study that posited a connection between the attenuated measles virus in MMR vaccine and autism, and surrounding thimerosal, a mercury derivative, rates of exemptions received increased scrutiny by researchers who warned that more exemptions might lead to lower vaccination rates, damaging herd immunity (New and Senior). Over the decades to follow, this would come to be true in many parts of Southern California, where some school districts would maintain low rates of vaccination while others would remain high, and across the region, researchers and public health officials warned that vaccination rates needed to remain even higher for herd immunity to be maintained in some instances (Salmon et al., "Health Consequences"; Salmon et al., "Public Health"; Atwell et al.; Buttenheim). Therefore, immediately preceding the Disneyland outbreak, the rhetorical landscape was inflected with vigorous local tensions over the importance of herd immunity, parent choice, and the need to vaccinate.

In this section, I discuss responses across media reporting on the outbreak and the ways in which discourses were constrained by the material exigence of eradication. The examples I analyze show how eradication, both when explicitly invoked and when alluded to in discourse, creates and constrains public responses to the outbreak. Three factors make such constraint especially apparent in this case: the construction of measles as a once-eliminated disease that was nearly eradicated prior to increases in exemptions, the existing local conflicts over exemptions that could damage eradication attempts, and existing criticisms of parents who were damaging the reputation—and thus eradication potential—of vaccines through their choice not to vaccinate.

Accommodating a Scourge "Once Eliminated"

Protecting the community and keeping overall disease incidents and risks low are important components of vaccination that also drive and heighten tension concerning vaccination. In much of the reporting about Disneyland, the idea of eradication was invoked directly as a promise of vaccination that was being jeopardized by noncompliance with vaccination recommendations. This was primarily done by characterizing measles as something that was "once eliminated," an argument that posited the outbreak as evidence that measles was no longer eliminated because of vaccine refusal and rising numbers of PBEs.

Noting that measles was once declared eliminated in the US was a constant refrain across reporting on the epidemic. Such invocations ranged from the mild statement of fact that "while measles was declared eliminated from the United States in 2000, the illness has reappeared in recent years, brought in from overseas and transmitted to Americans who did not get vaccinated" (AP), to statements that sought to amplify the crisis, such as the following that appeared in the *New York Times*:

> Measles anxiety rippled thousands of miles beyond its center on Friday as officials scrambled to try to contain a wider spread of the highly contagious disease—which America declared vanquished 15 years ago, before a statistically significant number of parents started refusing to vaccinate their children. (Healy and Paulson)

The statement above functions as an almost perfect example of the epideictic rhetoric that permeated reporting about the outbreak—praising the power of vaccinations to eliminate disease in America while casting blame upon a specific culprit: the "statistically significant number of parents" who refused vaccines.

Although a powerful response to eradication, often little distinction was made in reporting between popular and scientific or public health definitions of elimination. Modern public health efforts in response to disease range from control to elimination to eradication, making elimination an important point along the trajectory to eradication (Molyneux et al.). Elimination, in technical terms, "denote[s] the cessation of transmission of an organism throughout a country or region. . . . Like control, elimination is location-specific and would require ongoing interventions to be sustained in order to prevent reemergence of the disease from microbe importations" (Miller et al., "Control" 1165). Specifically, the CDC defines measles elimination as the "absence of continuous disease transmission for 12 months or more in a specific geographic area" (CDC, "Measles FAQs"). This statement goes on to clarify that despite notable occasional epidemics, as of 2018 measles still qualified as eliminated since it remained relatively uncommon, was not transmitted widely, and was not endemic to the US (CDC, "Measles"). Therefore, despite reporting that indicated otherwise, the epidemic was not evidence that measles was no longer eliminated or that the epidemic had somehow changed its status.

Scholars have pointed out that *elimination,* although a formal designation, can be a problematic term, especially when used popularly. Popularly, elimination can connote a disease that is simply within acceptable thresholds, is not a threat, or is synonymous with eradication, although, as stated above, elimination actually has formal boundaries beyond these popular perceptions (Miller, Barnett, and Henderson 1165). Such a scenario recalls the observations of Jeanne Fahnestock in the deontological and teleological accommodations of science in popular reporting. As Fahnestock observes, deontological accommodations associate scientific findings with praise, hope, and "wonder" beyond even scientists' intentions; teleological accommodations posit future applications and possibilities for findings that may or may not be commensurate with those findings ("Accommodating Science" 279). In the case of elimination, for the media, the idea that measles was the "once-eliminated" disease served as a powerful point of amplification of the consequences of vaccination refusal, offering both deontological and teleological accommodations, imagining that "elimination" signified future, hopeful possibilities for disease beyond what the term actually meant to experts.

Frank Bruni's op-ed in the *New York Times* offers another useful example of how elimination was used in popular reporting and arguments about the outbreak:

> In 2004, there were just 37 reported cases of measles in the United States. In 2014, there were 644. And while none of those patients died, measles can kill. Before vaccines for it became widespread in 1963, millions of Americans were infected annually, and 400 to 500 died each year.

This statement makes a series of before-and-after arguments that indicate a regression regarding the nation's vulnerability to measles, contrasting a historic low in measles cases in 2004 with an increase by 2014, and finally harking back to 1963, when the measles vaccine was first released. Bruni's argument is that lax vaccination practices over a decade were sending us on a trajectory back to a time when measles didn't just infect four hundred people but killed that same number and sickened millions more. Stating that one outbreak of measles was jeopardizing such success functions as a rhetorically powerful invocation of how exemptions and refusal jeopardize eradication efforts. However, Bruni's use of the 2014 number of cases of measles obscures the specifics of that data point. Although this number (644 cases of measles) is correct, the rise in measles cases in 2014 is largely attributed to an outbreak of measles in a predominantly unvaccinated Amish community in Ohio. In this specific case, two members of the community visited the Philippines, where measles is endemic and where they were experiencing a local outbreak. The men returned to their community, and their families and local community members were quickly infected, although there was little exposure outside the community (Gastañaduy). As a community, the Amish "limit participation in preventive health care, which results in low immunization rates and an increased risk of vaccine-preventable diseases" (Gastañaduy 1344). Although serious, there are different factors and extenuating circumstances associated with the 2014 spike that go beyond the number of PBEs filed in California, which is the thrust of the argument that Bruni is making in this piece.

Rhetorically, the use of elimination throughout the reporting serves as a way of responding to material exigencies of eradication created by vaccines. Elimination, popularly, was used to connote eradication—or at least its possibilities—even if that isn't what it technically meant to the experts who define the concept. Consequently, the outbreak was cast as an example of how the possibilities and benefits of eradication were slipping away. This argument was also one way that the media focused blame for the event on a specific public health concern: personal belief exemptions.

Enthymemes and Exemptions

PBEs had long been a source of concern for public health officials and the media in Southern California.[9] Specifically in the months leading up to the outbreak, the argument that vaccination rates in Southern California were lower than the South Sudan, and that exemptions were to blame for it, featured in the news cycle.

In September 2014, just a few months before the outbreak, the *Hollywood Reporter* published an article on recent cases of pertussis in California. The

---

9. Researchers have also long been concerned about the effect that high rates of PBEs might have on herd immunity for measles as well as for pertussis. In the years leading up to the Disneyland outbreak, cases of pertussis had increased; for example, in 2010 there were 9,120 cases of pertussis, causing many to grow increasingly concerned about the impact that PBEs were having on herd immunity and resulting rates of transmission (Atwell et al.). For a disease like pertussis, the situation is complicated by waning immunity; the acellular vaccine currently administered against pertussis does not have the same long-term immunity as the previous whole-cell variety administered through the 1980s. However, as elective nonvaccination rises, this contributes to a waning of herd immunity at the local level, exposing a community to more disease risk.

article featured an interactive map that allowed readers to find the enrollment, vaccination, and vaccine exemption rates for schools in California. The article's argument consisted of a series of premises and conclusions exemplified in statements such as "Vaccination rates are plummeting at top Hollywood schools, from Malibu to Beverly Hills, from John Thomas Dye to Turning Point, where affluent, educated parents are opting out in shocking numbers (leaving some schools' immunization rates on par with South Sudan) as an outbreak of potentially fatal whooping cough threatens L.A. like 'wildfire'" (Baum). Such an argument relies on the syllogism of community immunity where

> High rates of exemptions equal low rates of vaccination
> Low rates of vaccinations create risk for disease
> Exemptions must be removed to prevent incidents of disease

However, the medico-legal rhetoric of such claims was fully facilitated via enthymeme, or an argument that relies on an unstated assumption that is shared or invoked among the intended audience to reach its intended conclusion.[10] In the case of the "immunization rates on par with South Sudan" argument, unstated assumptions about race, privilege, and responsibility work not to just blame exemptions for incidents of disease but to cast blame for jeopardizing eradication on the people who sought them. The larger, medico-legal rhetoric of these arguments operates enthymematically, making a series of arguments about vaccination and PBEs, where (1) vaccination rates were decreasing, as a consequence of increasing rates of PBEs; (2) PBEs are sought by "affluent, educated" parents of children at schools in wealthy areas; and that (3) these wealthy, educated parents are to blame for putting Southern Californians at disease risk—in this specific case, risks similar to those of South Sudan. The unstated assumption embedded in this argument is that such a situation—vaccination rates low as South Sudan—is undesirable, since the South Sudan is portrayed as a negative point of comparison.

However, a quick review of WHO data and reporting on vaccination rates in the region alone tells a complicated story about available statistics on vac-

---

10. In *From Hysteria to Hormones*, Amy Koerber offers a recent history of rhetoric's understanding of enthymeme, characterizing its current predominant understanding as a "gentle, yet forceful, rhetorical movement" (158). Specifically, Koerber states, "An enthymeme is effective in situations in which the audience is inclined—for any number of reasons—to accept the argument without the piece, or pieces, that are left unstated. Thus, an enthymeme can be any element in an argument that is not strictly rational but is powerful despite this lack of rationality (or perhaps because of it)" (159). The tacit, yet persuasive, nature of what goes unsaid in the "vaccination rates as low as South Sudan" argument is particularly potent in this case.

cination rates, reliability of data, and volatility of health care in the region. As the 2017 WHO report on DTP (equivalent to DTaP in the US, which protects against tetanus, diphtheria, and pertussis) states about the 2016 estimated rates,

> The Republic of South Sudan continues to be challenged by ongoing civil conflict in several states. Population displacements both internally and across international borders continues to be problematic with more than an estimated one million South Sudanese projected to be refugees in neighboring countries (UNHCR). Not surprisingly given the current situation, concerns continue with regards to quality of recording and monitoring, timeliness and completeness of data. Reported administrative coverage data reflect reporting from 80 percent of total expected district reports. WHO and UNICEF encourage continued efforts to improve recording and monitoring while also increasing coverage. (WHO, "South Sudan" 3)

Under such conditions, vaccination numbers are unsurprisingly unstable and low as a result of many factors, geopolitical, economic, and cultural. The WHO report on vaccination coverage reveals wide variability in vaccination coverage in 2014, with government official vaccination estimates at 72 percent, which are contradicted by WHO estimates closer to 50 percent. Yet these complexities, struggles, and uncertainties are obscured within the enthymematic shorthand of such arguments as those in the *Hollywood Reporter* article. In other words—we don't really even know what the vaccination rate in the South Sudan is, so to use it as a straw man for "low vaccination rates" or undesirable levels of uptake is argumentatively specious, relying on the negative connotations of a country in turmoil with inaccurate vaccination numbers, all used for the epideictic purposes of placing blame on the behaviors of parents and praising medico-legal power of vaccine policies.

A further unstated assumption is that rates of exemptions in California could be equated with overall rates of vaccination, which does not consistently bear out in the data. For example, the original *Hollywood Reporter* data showed "high risk" schools like Canyon Elementary reporting that 34 percent of its students had filed PBEs, but vaccination rates for DTaP were at 66 percent, indicating that more students had exemptions than were actually using them for all vaccines. In this case, even if we were to compare vaccination rates at this elementary school with those in the South Sudan, vaccination rates are still higher than WHO estimates. But the enthymeme's unstated assumptions work to elide all of these key nuances to the situation. Hence, analysis of the enthymemic construction of this argument demonstrates how these unstated assumptions "move" the argument toward a conclusion that exemptions should be removed, making a medico-legal argument in service of eradication by deploying problematic connections across the data (Koerber, *Hysteria* 158).

All told, these arguments come together to connect PBEs with higher rates of outbreaks and risk to communities. As with the case of arguments about elimination, arguments about exemptions offer a specific way in which the material exigence of eradication is responded to in vaccine discourses. Exemptions function as a specific pathway through which the objectives of eradication are jeopardized. Even though media constructions of that jeopardy are often imprecise, relying on unstated assumptions or false equivalencies to become persuasive, rhetorically they function epideictically—to place blame for a phenomenon onto a specific practice, or on the exemption.

The final trope extends that blame to a particular group of parents— vaccine refusers in general and Jenny McCarthy in particular.

Science versus Jenny McCarthy

A February 2015 broadcast of the show *Live with Jimmy Kimmel* featured a satirical public service announcement (PSA) that offers an emblematic articulation of one of the major themes that emerged during the outbreak: frustration that people would believe "anti-vax" ideas propagated by Jenny McCarthy over doctors and science.

The PSA features a cast of six doctors who state things like "I am a doctor . . . And I believe in vaccinations . . . there is basically no reason to not vaccinate your kids . . . which is why I cannot fucking believe we have to make this PSA" (Kimmel). In Kimmel's introduction, he concludes that the measles epidemic is the fault of "antivaccine people":

> I know if you're one of these antivaccine people you probably aren't going to take medical advice from a talk show host . . . But I would expect you to take medical advice from almost every doctor in the world. See the thing about doctors is they didn't learn the human body from their friend's Facebook page. They went to medical school where they studied all sorts of amazing things like how to magically prevent children from contracting horrible diseases by giving them a little shot. . . . But some people do not buy into that because they did a Google search and Jenny McCarthy popped up and she had clothes on so they listened to what she had to say and decided not to vaccinate their kids. ("Viola Davis")

Kimmel's segment reflects many of the questions people had and assumptions they made about the nature of vaccine skepticism: Why would some people question vaccination? Why do some people still think MMR vaccine causes autism even though the study that posited that connection was fraudulent? Why would anyone believe Jenny McCarthy—a former *Playboy* playmate who has asserted that vaccines caused her son's autism—over the swaths of doctors, scientists, and public health officials who claim the contrary?

McCarthy, through her role as a mother-advocate and vocal opponent of vaccinations, has long been a lightning rod for criticism among vaccine advocates. McCarthy is probably the most popular vocal opponent of vaccination, although she is far from alone among celebrities who have questioned vaccines. Jim Carrey, for instance, has been incredibly vocal in his critiques of vaccines and joined Jenny McCarthy in much of her activism during their five-year relationship. Robert De Niro has been a vocal public skeptic of vaccines. Oprah Winfrey also has controversial views on vaccinations, in addition to a number of other scientific issues, and gave McCarthy a platform for an extensive interview on vaccine injuries in 2007. However, it is McCarthy who personally receives the most derision.[11]

McCarthy was invoked repeatedly throughout the epidemic and ensuing aftermath. The *Economist* reported on the outbreak in January in the article "Of Vaccines and Vacuous Starlets," featuring a large picture of McCarthy at the outset of the article and tracing decreased herd immunity to her popularization of the debunked MMR–autism link. The *LA Times* article "Jenny McCarthy: Public Menace" outlines her past claims about MMR and autism, comments on communicable disease, and her son's autism as a background for an article otherwise entirely about the outbreak. The article connects her role in promoting "antivaccination beliefs" to diminishing public confidence in vaccination and thus the outbreak. A rabbi penned a piece in the online Jewish magazine *Tablet* entitled "If Jenny McCarthy Were Jewish, She'd Have to Vaccinate," which ultimately argues that it is one's moral responsibility to the community to vaccinate one's children. Articles that did not lead with her image or feature her name in their titles still invoked her somewhere in the discussion of the outbreak, such as this quotation from a report on the out-

11. For example, there is the *Jenny McCarthy Body Count* website and *StopJenny.com,* which blame McCarthy for incidents of vaccine-preventable disease and deaths. There's a song called "The Jenny McCarthy Song," widely circulated on vaccine advocacy and science websites and blogs, which juxtaposes images of sick children with popular images of McCarthy from celebrity events and compares her to Susan Smith, who was convicted for murdering her children in 1995. And McCarthy is frequently mentioned in books, articles, and interviews by vaccine experts as promoting "bad science" and creating the problem of antivaccinationism. This was especially the case in the immediate reporting on the Disneyland outbreak.

break by Al Jazeera America: "The measles outbreak sheds light on a growing anti-vaccination movement, spread by parents and advocates, including
former ABC television host Jenny McCarthy. As a result, parents may opt
not to immunize their children because of religious beliefs or the fear that
vaccines are linked to developmental problems such as autism" (Taylor).
Interestingly enough, McCarthy never inserted herself publicly into this controversy, despite her numerous mentions across reporting. This was noted in
one article, entitled "Measles Are Back, But Where Is Jenny McCarthy?" which
described her deafening silence on the issue. She didn't hold press confer-
ences. She didn't comment. She didn't even participate in protests against the
resulting SB 277, which removed PBEs. In reality, she wasn't a part of the issue
at all, but she still factors prominently in media reporting. Even the articles
that featured her and her name most prominently did so to only remote rhetorical effect—McCarthy's small actual role in the outbreak itself made her a
distant, scant connection to the real news of the article, reporting on the outbreak, new danger zones, and other relevant concerns.

Jenny McCarthy's strange role in the media about the outbreak demonstrates, rhetorically, how important McCarthy is to contemporary arguments
about the importance of vaccination. McCarthy functions as something
between a straw man and a scapegoat for all of vaccine refusal, skepticism,
and concern. She is convenient because she possesses no scientific creden-
tials to be influential about vaccinations, and she even characterizes herself
as a "mother-warrior" with no particular scientific training and a "degree
from the University of Google" (Schlussel). She is easy to ridicule because
her comments are often ridiculous. She has advocated dangerous "alternative"
therapies meant to "cure" autism. She has advocated for the return of measles
with casual disregard for the many people for whom that would be a death
sentence (Offit, *Deadly Choices*). Her history as a *Playboy* playmate, bawdy
humor, and exaggerated affect all make her the perfect person to stand in for
vaccine skepticism, if one wants to diminish that view. She is beautiful to look
at and easy to make fun of.

Bringing up McCarthy also makes for a rhetorically convenient way to
reify the value of science in the face of even seemingly widespread popular
resistance to vaccinations. To align McCarthy with all vaccine skeptics is to
put her beliefs into direct opposition with the power and value of science itself.
Crafting an "us versus them" scenario, where "us" are scientific experts taking
on the noble goal of eradicating disease and "them" are foolish, unthinking,
uncaring, bimbos. Such reification signals the public health imperative to vaccinate and material exigence of eradication by making claims of skepticism
ultimately invalid when represented by such an inadequate public figure.

MEDICO-LEGAL RHETORICS AND
EXIGENCIES OF ERADICATION

Since the development of the measles vaccine and adoption of widespread vaccine mandates, measles has been regarded as a prime candidate for eradication through vaccination efforts (Conis, *Vaccine Nation* 7). Yet rates of uptake have hampered efforts to achieve this vision, for many reasons: issues with accessibility and availability of the vaccine, public apathy about the seriousness of measles, and vaccine controversies surrounding the MMR vaccine, particularly through the late 1990s. Despite vocal opposition to the MMR vaccine, eradication stands firm as a material exigence—a material result (extinction of disease) that demands response.

As medico-legal rhetorics, media discourses concerning the Disneyland outbreak respond to this exigence often through of epideictic rhetoric, using various argumentative constructions to cast blame for continued disease onto those who refuse to vaccinate, but also using accommodation tactics and problematic enthymemic constructions that advance conclusions about vaccine uptake, vaccine rates, and vaccine policies that obscure the complicated ways in which the situation operates. By accommodating the notion of elimination, the media response reifies the power that vaccines have had over diseases like measles, enabling typically low levels of measles cases every year. Enthymemes move through reporting, relying upon unstated assumptions about nonvaccinators, disease, and the imperative of eradiation to "blame" particular actors for the crisis. As the appeal to remove exemptions intensifies, these rhetorics assign blame to exemptions in general, and to "stupid" parents who pursue them in particular, thereby assigning responsibility to everyone to help achieve the goal of eradication. Under such conditions, those who seek exemptions are subject to particular criticism and scrutiny; hence the persistent references to Jenny McCarthy despite her lack of public involvement with the outbreak. Such a move, rhetorically, aligns parents who seek exemptions with an unsympathetic, illegitimate public actor who jeopardizes us all. Each construction uses the power of medicine and law to construct praise for benevolent actors and actions, to blame those who are at fault, and to assign the appropriate, regulatory path forward.

In so doing, these reports respond to and reflect the power of the material exigence of eradication to drive discourse and discord. Exemptions *do* jeopardize vaccine success (Salmon et al., "Health Consequences"; Salmon et al., "Public Health"; Atwell et al.; Wang et al.; Feikin et al.; Shaw et al.), and more disease *does* put more vulnerable people at risk. Consequently, eradication and exemptions are locked in opposition, exemptions functioning as a key way through which eradication efforts can be undermined. Casting measles as "once eliminated" and describing any incident of measles as jeopardizing that status situates eradication itself as a precarious state that needs to be protected by strict boundaries at the level of the community, regarding what diseases are permitted, where, and under what conditions. This is what eradication as a material exigence does—it sets an expectation that incidents of vaccine-preventable disease are unacceptable, as are any measures that jeopardize the possibility of eradication. Such a situation strips the situation of its rhetoricity, offering regulatory, compulsory measures as the only path to eradication if people will not electively comply with recommendations. Mandates, free of nonmedical exemptions, are the only option to which all discourses drive.

OBJECTION AND THE GREATER GOOD

As eradication is reconsidered not simply as a public health goal or as a key possibility of vaccination but as a material exigence, demanding response from audiences discussing vaccines, the role it plays in motivating and perpetuating conflict about vaccines becomes clearer. Any discussion about vaccination is not simply about the vaccination itself—its health benefits to individuals or families or communities—but is also a democratic, deliberative question about policy and what vaccines *can* and *should* be allowed to do to individuals, families, and communities. Because vaccines are not about protecting individuals alone, they are essentially community products that involve community decision-making.

Thus, vaccines have enormous power to shape disease at the level of populations, but only if entire populations comply—or are compelled to comply—with mass vaccination efforts. Such an effort is inherently rhetorically challenging. Social conditions where everyone agrees that the exact same thing should happen at the exact same time and is entirely beneficial and consequence-free to everyone are rare. Clearly, such a moment existed in the mid-twentieth century as smallpox eradication efforts were undertaken, but such a situation has arguably not existed since. Vaccines *do* carry the real possibility of injury, after all, and as the next chapter discusses, actors across the issue use discourse in a variety of ways to argue that these injuries are not only more frequent but more severe than health officials will acknowledge.

This tension, between the capabilities of the vaccine as an object and its ability to injure in both authorized and unauthorized forms, makes the exemption a particularly contentious space in contemporary vaccine debates, which is why it caused so much conflict following the 2014 Disneyland outbreak. As the next chapter discusses, the exemption is a linchpin in the exigence of injury, giving concerned parents a mechanism for exacting choice despite powerful material exigencies that demand disease prevention and eradication. At the same time, however, the exemption is the Achilles' heel of eradication efforts—the one thing that could undermine the entire effort. If left unaddressed, these opposing material exigencies will always produce conflict, as mandates and exemptions mediate, often without acknowledging, these contradictory positions.

CHAPTER 3

Family, Authority, Injury

W. J. FURNIVAL, a nineteenth-century antivaccination activist, describes the conscientious objector[1] to vaccination as a

> parent residing in England, who, by reason of certain mild or bitter experiences of his own, by observing what has occurred in other families, by studying the special investigations of gifted scientific men, and by personal "bed-rock" inquiry into the real nature of vaccine itself, has become so firmly convinced of the futility, repulsiveness, and dangers of the operation of vaccination, that he cannot, as a devoted and intelligent parent, conscientiously consent, to subject the beloved children of whom he is natural protector to such a rite. (Durbach 175)

The National Vaccine Information Center (NVIC)—a nonprofit group that fights vaccine mandates and promotes "vaccine choice"—notes the following on its website today:

---

1. In the nineteenth century, those who protested compulsory vaccination of children against smallpox used the concept of the "conscientious objection" to advocate for laws that would protect parents who did not want their children vaccinated from mandatory statutes that often carried substantial fines or imprisonment for noncompliance.

We as parents, who know and love our children better than anyone else, we, by U.S. law and a larger moral imperative, are the guardians of our children until they are old enough to make life and death decisions for themselves. . . . We are their voice and by all that is right in this great country and in the moral universe, we should be allowed to make a rational, informed, voluntary decision about which diseases and which vaccines we are willing to risk their lives for—without fearing retribution from physicians employed by the state.

Argue with us. Educate us. Persuade us. But don't track us down and force us to violate our moral conscience. (Loe Fisher)

Although over a century separates these manifestos, the concept of conscience, of rational, reasoned protest to vaccination and the laws that mandate it, figures prominently in both. As these manifestos articulate, the position of these parents is that they have the right to retain the power to refuse vaccinations on behalf of their children to protect them from the risks of vaccination. To what risks, exactly, do these parents and patients refer, though? Embedded in these discourses and rhetorics separated by space, place, and time is *injury,* the material exigence examined in this chapter. In both of these cases, injury functions as the central exigence to which these calls for objection respond. More than the specific concerns of MMR and autism (though these are embedded in skepticisms in contemporary debates), injuries consist of real threats of bodily injury, and parents perceive themselves as charged with protecting their children from these threats.

In so doing, the parents and patients who raise these questions interrogate dominant notions about what constitutes vaccine-related risks, valid forms of evidence, and the role of professional and scientific knowledge in decisions about vaccine mandates. As parents respond to the exigence of injury, they invoke and reify vaccine-skeptical arguments made by texts like the 2012 book *Vaccine Epidemic: How Corporate Greed, Biased Science, and Coercive Government Threaten Our Human Rights, Our Health, and Our Children,* which articulates a wide range of concerns about vaccination that transcend concerns about vaccines and autism. These concerns include charges against the constitutionality of mandatory vaccination laws, questioning of the inherent risks of vaccination as a violation of informed consent, and skepticisms about the financial incentives for pharmaceutical companies.[2] All told, these arguments

---

2. In this text, Louise Kuo Habakus and Mary Holland adopt the term *vaccine choice* in an effort to avoid the "pro" and "anti" vaccination language in which vaccine positions are typically characterized. This position underscores their aim to reshape the discussion into a debate about what parents and patients should be able to choose to do with their bodies, not about

offer evidence in support of maintaining vaccine exemptions so that parents may choose, on a case-by-case, vaccine-by-vaccine basis, which possibilities for injury they want to accept for themselves and their families.

This chapter primarily examines the discourses that parents and patients have produced online to respond to the material exigence of *injury* through material rhetorics of presence and confession. Using principles of rhetorical presence and the truth-making power of confession, they materialize and substantiate their charges of injury in what I am calling *vaccine injury confessionals* posted online. These authors forgo privacy and anonymity in order to give firsthand accounts of their vaccine injuries (most of which have not been validated by vaccine courts or other authorities). Responding to public rebuke of the authors' experiences, vaccine injury confessionals present an embodied, visceral claim: look at what the vaccine did to me or my child. Instead of preventing disease, vaccines produced injury, according to these rhetors, responding to the material exigence of injury as a prominent, profound imperfection of vaccination. Injury functions therefore as an important antagonist, because injury informs and heightens the material qualities of vaccination inherent in the vaccine's material operation.

This chapter begins by discussing the operation of injury as a material exigence in vaccination, establishing how rhetorical presence, rhetorical authority, and confession offer mechanisms through which the materialities of injury are responded to, articulated, and amplified. Then, through a discussion of established research and examples of injury confessions online, I discuss how the concept of rhetorical presence in particular explains why these discourses function as powerful forms of response to material exigencies of injury.

MATERIAL EXIGENCE: VACCINATION
AND THE THREAT OF INJURY

Vaccines are injurious in ways that are authorized and not authorized by the dominant discourses of science and medicine, meaning that injury, at some

the validity of vaccination as a practice per se. The book functions largely as an attempt to legitimize Habakus and Holland's discourse in an effort to make vaccine choice an acceptable, even logical, practice in an ethical society. By including lesser-heard legal arguments, cultural critiques regarding the nature of health and wellness in current practices in pediatrics, and calls for more scientific research into possible reasons for unexpected adverse reactions to vaccines (such as genetic predispositions to certain diseases that may make some patients more prone to complications), Habakus and Holland paint a very different picture of the nature and bases of their arguments. Far from the nonsensical rantings of denialists, each essay attempts a linkage between itself and a dominant discourse, be it science or law or even contemporary ethics.

level, must be realized, accepted, and dealt with during vaccination. After all, what is a vaccine, to the individual, other than an injury? Under the best of conditions, two forms of physical injury occur—a needle pierces skin and perhaps muscle, and then a serum is injected into the body that contains a whole host of ingredients, including adjuvants and microbial materials, designed to ignite an immune response. A little bit of blood, mild fever, cries in an infant or child (or adult, depending), and moderate discomfort are nearly certain to follow. Fainting, high fevers, and seizures are perhaps less likely but not uncommon reactions to the experience of being vaccinated. This does not count the incredibly rare but still very possible serious adverse events possible following vaccination, including life-altering disabilities and death.

Despite these authorized forms of injury, vaccines are still described as safe, in that they typically do not cause injuries that outweigh the risks of the diseases they are designed to prevent. Serious side effects are exceedingly rare. The US has federal systems in place for tracking and responding to adverse reactions to vaccines.[3] And in the past when safety has been an issue, immediate, swift steps were taken to recall and cease vaccine administration until problems were resolved. Most notably, this includes the following: in 1955 over 200,000 children and adults were afflicted with paralytic polio resulting from improperly inactivated vaccine distributed by Cutter Laboratories (Offit, *Cutter*); in

---

3. We have routinized mechanisms for mediating vaccine risks in the US. In addition to lengthy trials and high standards maintained by the scientific, medical, and public health communities prior to approval of a vaccine, a number of public structures are in place to help mitigate vaccine risks. We maintain the Vaccine Adverse Event Reporting (VAERS) system to maintain surveillance over vaccine adverse reactions following their licensure and deployment. The National Vaccine Injury Compensation Program (VICP) is funded by the public and is responsible for assessing vaccine injuries and compensating those determined to have been injured by vaccines for their injury-related expenses. These systems began in the 1980s and early 1990s, following the National Vaccine Injury Act of 1986, which sought to protect health care providers and vaccine makers from liability in the case of a vaccine injury, which, lawmakers feared, would discourage them from creating and administering vaccines. In the event that someone experiences serious injuries from a vaccine, he or she is not able, as is the case with other drugs, to seek compensation from the manufacturer of the vaccine or the person who administered it but rather must seek compensation from the VICP. A VICP panel assesses the person's injury and awards compensation based on that assessment. The most recent Vaccine Injury Table—which outlines the specific conditions and reactions that are eligible for compensation—lists everything from immediate anaphylaxis and shock from a vaccine to encephalopathy, vaccine-strain measles infection, thrombocytopenic purpura, and intussusception among the most serious injuries eligible for compensation. Although these instances are exceedingly rare and are often associated with other comorbidities that will increase risk (vaccine strain measles infection, for instance, is associated with patients who are already immune-deficient), they are risks nonetheless that we all assume and work to mitigate through a variety of measures associated with vaccination.

1976 the National Influenza Immunization Program (NIIP) was initiated after a soldier at Fort Dix, in New Jersey, died of swine flu in an effort to pre-empt a possible highly infectious pandemic. In the end, no additional cases of swine flu were confirmed nationwide, but forty million Americans were vaccinated, and thirty-two people died of Guillain–Barré syndrome, a neurological disorder, as a result of the vaccine ("1976 Swine Flu Outbreak Ford Administration Papers"). Finally, the rotavirus vaccine Rotashield was no longer recommended for use in infants on October 22, 1999, after being licensed in August 1998. Rotashield was found to result in increased risk of developing intussusception (a condition where a segment of intestine, usually at the ileocecal sphincter [the site where the large and small intestines join], folds in on itself, causing a blockage), twenty to thirty times over expected risk in otherwise healthy infants (CDC, "Rotavirus Vaccine").

However, charges of other forms of injury that are not authorized by scientific and medical authorities remain prominent across discussion about vaccinations because they operate as a material exigence, one created by the vaccine itself but also extended and sustained through the materiality of injured bodies, recounted online. These injuries range from generalized toxicity (through the injection of chemicals and unnatural ingredients directly into the bloodstream) to neurological or physiological effects (which could range from something as specific as autism to general behavioral issues, gastrointestinal [GI] problems, weakening of the immune system, or other impediments to growth and development) to evolutionary and population-wide consequences (such as contributing to the development of new or antibiotic- or antiviral-resistant strains of bacteria and viruses). Some of these narratives make the charge that a vaccine caused autism, but as the examples in this chapter show, this argument is one among many that respond to the exigence of injury. Furthermore, these concerns do not just respond to established vaccine side effects—the claims involve longer-term injuries inflicted on individual bodies and whole communities that, according to a range of beliefs and perspectives, are either unknown or unacknowledged by the medical-industrial-governmental complex that produces and recommends vaccines.

Ultimately, claims of injury that are not validated by science use a set of rhetorics that establish and reify the exigence of injury in ways that are persuasive to many, despite their lack of access to dominant systems and forms of power that could officially validate them. One key way in which this happens is by establishing *rhetorical authority* and *rhetorical presence* through the confessional form, which works potently with contemporary instantiations of vaccine controversy and online media to respond to material exigencies.

Rhetorical Authority and Rhetorical Presence

Michael McGee and John Lyne observe that rhetorical and Platonic models of authority come into conflict in controversies where expert or specialized discourses are deliberated and decided upon by the lay public at large. Platonic authority comes from expert forms of knowledge, such as medical and scientific discourses. Platonic authority functions as a "chaste rhetoric that pretends not to be rhetorical" but in so doing fails to persuade individuals who may not be motivated to act by expert knowledge alone ("Nice Folks" 393). McGee and Lyne posit a second kind of authority, rhetorical authority, where "credible experts, on the rhetorical model of authority, must facilitate the act of judgment—that is, they must speak that language of knowledge which translates easily into the language of action and promotes a fusion of the two" (391). Expert knowledge that demands compliance "because the doctor says so," as with vaccination, can be less persuasive because of its lack of rhetorical authority among some parents—it functions with Platonic authority rather than rhetorical authority. In the context of a medical decision, for some individuals, scientific expertise or the doctor's advice alone does not always convince—it is convincing only as part of a complex of authority that facilitates decision-making.

As it relates to material exigence specifically, rhetorical presence is an important avenue to creating counterarguments to dominant medical and scientific discourses, in response to the exigence of injury. Such a response includes a second significant rhetorical tactic—the *rhetorical presence* of the child and the child's body as evidence of injury and illness—that this appeal to ethos necessitates. Chaim Perelman and Lucie Olbrechts-Tyteca's notion of rhetorical presence proposes how presence might be established and constructed. For Perelman and Olbrechts-Tyteca, rhetorical presence is a "technique of concretization in argument" (358) where "an element has presence by virtue of its inclusion in an argument, and this inclusion implies the element's 'pertinency' and 'importance' to the situation" (359). Presence is also amplified by rhetorical tactics such as "the strategic accumulation of detail to convey 'an impression of reality,' and the use of 'concrete terms' to give an element presence relative to those expressed in more abstract language" (361). In the case of the latter form of amplification, an element gains increased presence in an utterance as it becomes more real, tangible, and accessible to the audience.

Parents, patients, and other agents use rhetorical presence to challenge the rhetorical authority of dominant discourses that claim that vaccine injuries are rare or minor. To do so, these agents need some kind of evidentiary appeal. One significant way in which this is established, particularly in contemporary vaccine debates, is through confessional storytelling, which uses the episte-mological and ontological powers of the confessional mode to establish and respond to injuries caused by vaccines.

The Power(s) of Confession

In the case of responses to the material exigencies of injury in vaccination, rhetorical presence and authority are crafted discursively through confessional storytelling. Foucault calls confession "a ritual of discourse in which the speaking subject is also the subject of the statement; it is also a ritual that unfolds within a power relationship, for one does not confess without the presence (or virtual presence) of a partner who is not simply the interlocutor but the authority who requires the confession" (qtd in Bernstein 15). Here, Foucault outlines a few basic components of a confessional situation: it necessarily occurs in dialogue, where there is at least one speaker and one listener, and the purpose for the dialogue is the exchange of truths—of experiences on behalf of the speaker and interpretations and paths to absolution in the case of the listener.

St. Augustine's conception of confession and the Foucauldian view overlap in some ways, though Augustine's notion offers additional nuances to the discursive practice, mainly the idea of performativity. As Erik Doxtader writes, "For a very long time, the power of confession's truth(fulness) has been pegged to its performative quality. As Augustine suggested, the confession relies not only on what is said but the manner in which it is spoken, a way of speaking that reveals the damage done and which brings those suffering the weight of sin back into relation with the (true) word" (270). Here, in Doxtader's reading of Augustine, confession is a powerful discourse in its ability to be truth-producing and affirming. Furthermore, as David Tell maintains, for Augustine confession is a way of memorializing experience, of bringing the past into the present and preserving past acts. Tell writes, "Confession is a performative remembering in which the object of memory is not contained in the mind before it is disclosed through speech; rather, it is embodied in the speech act" (234). Confession is a performance, therefore, of past acts with the purpose of memorializing them for consideration in a present moment.

Kimberly Hall's observations on the use of confessional online pick up these notions as they are used in video-based confessionals in particular.[4] In

---

4. The community created in online spaces has been of significant interest to scholars in digital rhetorics as well. Angela Haas studied the phenomenon of online support communities formed to deal with another medical issue: infertility. People use online spaces to reclaim the

her study of "cue card confessionals," Hall notes that such confessionals produce truth not just through the confessional form but through the community
that such confessionals create in online spaces. Because the confessionals are
at once deeply personal, a revealing of self, and then made public through distribution on the internet, the confessional necessarily invites and engages the
audience to participate in the truth-making of the confessional act. Whether
by inviting the audience to acknowledge new forms of representation, the
marginalization of a social act or belief, or as a way of reclaiming agency
lost by an experience like bullying or sexual assault, the confessional requires
an audience to participate in the truth-telling experience (236). Furthermore,
adapting from Walter Ong and the connections between confession and auto-
ethnography, Hall states:

> Autoethnography is a process of witnessing that grants "the ability for par-
> ticipants and readers to observe and, consequently, better testify on behalf
> of an event, problem, or experience," creating a method by which the per-
> sonal has the power to become political. This formulation asserts that the
> process of both producing and viewing autoethnographic accounts is a form
> of "witnessing" that marks the validity of the event or experience itself, and
> the authority to stand as witness to it. (286–87)

Together, practices of rhetorical authority, presence, and confession function
as interlocking rhetorics necessary for responding to contemporary material
exigencies of injury in vaccination. In the contemporary debate about vaccines, injury is downplayed as a statistical rarity by vaccine advocates while
amplified as more common by vaccine skeptics. Given that vaccine support
comes with the weight of scientific and medical authority and power, rhetorical presence, established through confession's evidentiary nature, offers a
powerful counterresponse to the exigence of disease (claiming instead that

agency that biomedical discourses can deny them, mainly through the act of storytelling. Haas
found that "by sharing . . . experiences with infertility, or other reproductive health issues, and
then critiquing the hegemonic values that have surrounded reproductive technologies, we can
help to further represent the female experience in a more liberating and inclusive way" (79).
Furthermore, the online community helped women regain agency in circumstances where they
felt that they lacked a space in traditional medical discourses for their views and experiences to
be heard and garner credence. As a result, the online spaces gave women "a say in reproductive
technologies and how they affect women" (79). In this sense, Haas's online medical discourse
community uses the internet as a subversive, feminist space where "hegemonic values" are challenged in a more open and free way than can occur in a doctor's office. Similarly, Kelly Pender's
2012 "Genetic Subjectivity in Situ: A Rhetorical Reading of Genetic Determinism and Genetic
Opportunity in the Biosocial Community of FORCE" examines how communities designed to
support people at genetic risk of various conditions develop and organize "pre-vivors" online.

risks *may* outweigh the benefits of preventing and eradicating disease) while responding to and establishing the exigence of injury at the same time. Such a method of response is unique to and critical for response in our contemporary moment; earlier generations of vaccine skeptics, as chapter 2 outlines, relied on local organization and opposition to vaccine mandates, which were also levied locally. With the combination of widespread vaccine mandates nationwide, distributed networking among vaccine skeptics, and the increasing power of science and the state to mandate health decisions, the internet combines twenty-first-century technologies, concerns, and communicative power to mount a significant counterargument to dominant discourses about vaccines and responses to material exigencies of injury.

Injury and the Internet

The immediate context for injury as a material exigence begins with a few key events of the past thirty years. In the late 1970s and 1980s, a parent group called Dissatisfied Parents Together (DPT) formed to demand changes to the whole-cell pertussis vaccination, which they believed had caused their children to experience severe reactions and lifelong disabilities when they received the vaccinations as children. These efforts ultimately culminated in two significant changes to both medicine and policy: a new, acellular pertussis vaccine that carried fewer side effects, and the National Vaccine Injury Act of 1986 (Offit, *Deadly Choices*). This law sought to protect health care providers and vaccine makers from liability in the case of a vaccine injury which, lawmakers feared, would discourage them from creating and administering vaccines. Specifically, the National Vaccine Injury Compensation Program (VICP) gave a mechanism for compensating those determined to have been injured by vaccines for their injury-related expenses. Vaccination rates were relatively stable through the '80s and early '90s, though lower than public health goals. Two factors were blamed for low vaccination rates: access—parents simply could not access or afford vaccinations—and the increasing sentiment that diseases that vaccinations protected against, such as measles and polio, were no longer a risk (Conis, *Vaccine Nation*).

Through the 1990s in the US, rates of vaccination—as well as the number and types of vaccines—rose substantially. Rising vaccination rates largely happened as a result of the Vaccines for Children program, a Clinton administration initiative (Conis, *Vaccine Nation* 163). Vaccines for Children provided financial aid to expand access to vaccines at a time when the set of recommended vaccines for infants, children, and adolescents was also increasing.

In the years following the beginning of Vaccines for Children in 1993, four vaccinations were added to the standard childhood schedule, and doses and boosters of existing vaccines increased.[5] As the new millennium approached, more children were getting more vaccinations more often, vastly expanding coverage and protection across new populations and against new diseases.[6] However, new concerns about vaccines were on the horizon. By the late 1990s, in conjunction with increasing vaccination dosages and the number of vaccines added to the schedule, three simultaneous events in very different public arenas occurred, reviving exigencies of injury and making voluntary nonvaccination a renewed problem.

The first event involved the removal of thimerosal from vaccinations in 1999, amid concerns that thimerosal might cause neurological problems in immunized children. Thimerosal contains ethylmercury, which is different than methylmercury, the well-known neurotoxin in fish that humans are advised to limit consumption of. However, in the late '90s, the safety of thimerosal came into question, when Congressman Robert Kennedy raised these concerns. The US Food and Drug Administration (FDA) reviewed thimerosal and concluded that the quantity of ethylmercury in vaccines exceeded Environmental Protection Agency (EPA) guidelines for infant exposure to

---

5. For context: in the 1983 vaccination schedule, children were vaccinated against seven diseases prior to age eighteen: diphtheria, pertussis, and tetanus (in one combined DTP vaccine); polio; and measles, mumps, and rubella (in one combined MMR vaccine). Those vaccines delivered eleven doses of vaccine from ages of two months to sixteen years. By 1989 just one other vaccine and dose was added: one dose of Hib vaccine, which protects against Haemophilus influenza B, at eighteen months. Beginning in the early 1990s, however, both the number of total diseases vaccinated against and the number of doses that children were given increased significantly. Four diseases were added to the schedule: hepatitis B vaccine in 1994, varicella in 1996, rotavirus in 1999, and hepatitis A in 2000 (as a recommendation, not a requirement, for all populations). By 2000 the total disease protection had expanded to eleven diseases administered over twenty-one vaccine doses, including a birth dose of hepatitis B, to be administered prior to hospital discharge (CDC, "Past Immunization Schedules").

6. This situation is important to understand from the perspective of the public as well as from the perspectives of scientists, doctors, and lawmakers. As Elena Conis points out in Vaccine Nation, through the mid-'90s, vaccines were perceived by politicians to be low-risk, high-reward ways to gain political favor among the public, since vaccines were largely for babies and young children, vaccine policies were relatively low-cost to implement, and vaccine policies received bipartisan support. So, despite a resurgence of vaccine hesitancy movements in the 1980s, lawmakers were mostly accustomed to vaccine expansion receiving widespread support. By contrast, for the vaccinating public, the increasingly frequent vaccine encounters were becoming complicating and confusing. It is during this period that studies show parents expressing concern about the quantity of vaccines as a rationale for refusing vaccinations. (Previous vaccine studies primarily found that parents thought that diseases like measles simply no longer carried risks as they had in previous generations.) And in the late 1990s and early 2000s, as controversies about vaccine ingredients began, the frequency with which vaccines had to be discussed during well-child visits certainly didn't seem to increase confidence in vaccination, given the controversies in the decades to come.

mercury, based on EPA guidelines on exposure to methylmercury (though it was, at that time, unclear whether ethylmercury carried the same risks). As a precaution, the FDA ordered the removal of thimerosal from vaccines (FDA, "Thimerosal in Vaccines"). At roughly the same time, in 1998, Andrew Wakefield published the now-infamous "Wakefield Study" in *The Lancet,* which posited a connection between the MMR vaccine and autism. The article described a small case study of twelve children whose parents reported the onset of autistic tendencies following the MMR vaccine (Wakefield et al.). Although the study was conducted in Britain, the story was widely reported in the American press and had a significant impact on concerns about vaccines in the US. Soon a wide range of concerns about vaccine ingredients, mercury, and development disorders began to grow and coalesce (Kolodziejski; Lerner). Third, and perhaps far less significantly than the previous two events, the rotavirus vaccine Rotashield was recalled in 1999. Rotashield had been connected to an increased rate of intussusception (a disorder where the intestine folds in on itself) (CDC, "Rotavirus Vaccine").

Although subsequent studies have shown no link between MMR and autism (Parker et al.; Andrews et al.; Price et al.), no evidence has demonstrated that ethylmercury poses the same dangers to humans as methylmercury, and a new rotavirus vaccine was released without the risk of intussusception (CDC, "Vaccines . . . Rotavirus"), this sequence of events together reignited the centuries-old exigence of injury concerning vaccination. Discord about injury and vaccines is only further amplified by online media that make stories of injury accessible across time, space, and social networks.

Studies of vaccine discourses on the internet in the 2000s reveal that injury grew as a powerful material exigence online in the decade immediately following these events. Ana Kata's 2010 analysis of website content describes themes of injury consistently operating across antivaccination websites, including questions about vaccination safety and effectiveness, such as charges that vaccines actually damage or hurt children's immune systems. In addition to these specific appeals or messages, Kata also found that parents often used emotive appeals, such as stories about children who were "damaged" by vaccines, and claims of "impartiality" as rhetorical tactics to establish validity and ethos.[7] Kata's 2012 study examines antivaccination sentiment on Web 2.0 content (now more commonly termed *social media*). Despite the

---

7. Kata also notes that these discourses challenge dominant notions about trust and authority, claiming that "traditional controversy dynamics, with 'audiences' needing to be 'educated' by 'experts,' no longer apply" (1715). Instead, expertise and authority are viewed with skepticism within the antivaccine discourse. Science is questioned, and appeals to expertise are seen as manipulative. Meanwhile, the "expertise" appeals of parents are rarely questioned, and their own appeals to scientism are often deployed in defense of antivaccine claims.

change in text for this analysis, however, Kata identifies a number of the same tropes related to injury, such as "You can't prove vaccines are safe," "Choosing between diseases and vaccine injuries," and "Science was wrong before," as common among the discourses shared on social media. Kata notes that these tactics and tropes are particularly effective because they are often masked in "unobjectionable rhetoric such as 'informed consent,' 'health freedom,' and 'vaccine safety'" (3784). Kata's studies are significant as they relate to injury as a material exigence for two primary reasons. First, across these studies of vaccine communication, injury remains omnipresent, directly emerging from the questions about vaccine injury in the public sphere in the 1990s. Whether these discourses make direct claims of injury or include adjacent arguments, such as those for maintaining mandates or arguing about the morality of animal testing, each response in some way both reifies and responds to the materiality of injury as an exigence that vaccines create. Second, Kata makes a number of conclusions about the inevitability of vaccine skepticism and its proliferation through social media and the internet, given their affordances in community-building and discursive power.

Significantly, Kata also concludes that although efforts to craft counter-messages online often try to offer legitimate alternatives to antivaccine messages, "an approach that moves beyond providing 'the facts' is likely needed. With the anti-vaccination movement embracing the postmodern paradigm, which inherently questions an authoritative, science-based approach, 'facts' may be reinterpreted as just another 'opinion'" (3784). Within a material exigence paradigm, this observation is pertinent and also self-evident: for persuasion to occur, exigencies must be acknowledged and modified. A response that is not informed by this exigence will undoubtedly fail to persuade. This is one reason why, for some agents across the debate, the individual story about an individual injury is more persuasive than large-scale, generalizable statistics about safety—the former discourse actually responds to the exigence of injury in a way that modifies, through further validation, the situation. In the next section, I discuss how discourses respond to exigencies of injury specifically through the personal stories of individuals who use online outlets to tell their narratives about the dangers of vaccines.

BEFORE-AND-AFTER: VACCINE INJURY CONFESSIONALS

Response to the material exigence of injury is articulated through a variety of discursive forms and media online; consequently, the examples examined here consist of confessional videos, written narratives, and memorials or tributes posted on websites. These texts attempt to demonstrate the dangers of vaccines by using images and stories of thriving, healthy bodies contrasted with the injured or frail bodies that remain after vaccine injury. These images and narratives attempt to show that vaccine injuries are more widespread, common, and serious than pharmaceutical companies, medical and public health professionals, and the government will acknowledge. Rhetorically, these narratives use the before-and-after argumentative structure to build rhetorical presence through the confessional form. The narratives relay the story of a healthy, functioning person (before), who is then vaccinated, and (after) harmed in an irrevocable way by that vaccine. Sometimes these stories are told by parents, sometimes they are self-authored; sometimes they are told in prose, others are created through video or pictorial slideshows; and still others are relayed through "memorials" offered online to "victims of the greater good." Gardasil and the flu vaccine, in addition to MMR and DTaP, are the vaccines with the most frequent charges of such injuries, though some narratives attribute injury and progressive developmental delays to "vaccines" writ large. Rhetorically, the before-and-after argument thus allows claims of injury in public discourses about vaccines to gain power because it uses the truth-making capacity of confession to establish the rhetorical presence of the injured body that results from vaccination.

The Persuasiveness of the Before-and-After Form

The following example articulates a claim of injury regarding Gardasil vaccine, posted on sanevax.org. Sanevax calls itself "the first international HPV vaccine information clearinghouse," promoting a range of stories about the dangers of vaccines in general, and HPV vaccines (most often Gardasil) in particular. The following narrative was contributed by a young woman and is representative of the before-and-after trope in injury confessionals:

> Prior to Gardasil, I had no previous known illnesses or behavioral issues, except for an occasional migraine headache . . . had my first Gardasil shot . . . on April 28, 2008. . . . My second Gardasil vaccination (Lot 0651X) was on January 8, 2009 and I had this along with a tetanus shot.
> My symptoms include: 30 lbs unexplained weight loss and my hair falling out in clumps and migraines. I experienced sudden sharp pains all over my body, which are most intense in my head, abdomen and legs. Earaches and frequent ear popping with pain and stiffness in elbows, knees, wrists and ankles and a numbness in my face including lips, nose and cheeks; pressure

in sinuses, stiffness and tightening in my neck. I have had vision problems including double vision, blurred vision, light auras, difficulty focusing and pain/pressure in and around my eyes. Frequent muscle spasms all over and a weakness/numbnes/tingling [*sic*] in arms and pains in legs.

Gardasil has completely changed my life. Before Gardasil, I never had a pain that I could not explain. For a year now I have been in and out of doctors' offices desperately searching for an answer. I am no longer able to perform my job the way I used to. Before Gardasil, I was enrolled in college with a 4.0 and now I cannot even finish a book I am just trying to enjoy. I feel like I am not giving my son and fiancé the time they deserve from me, because I am too tired, in too much pain, or because I am at the doctor's office. I just want to be myself again and enjoy every moment of being a mom, but everyday it feels like I am falling further away from the "old me" or the "me before Gardasil."

There are a few key, specific significant components of this narrative that work to build it as an argument that confesses vaccine injury. The person was healthy before the vaccination, signified through a pain-free, successful life full of academic achievement in college. In choosing to vaccinate, the speaker did not think she was doing something dangerous or risky and therefore didn't fully conceptualize possible risks. The vaccination functions as a nonspecific yet distinct injury that can be connected to vaccination; as a part of the narrative itself, this person does not report being injured by distinct ingredients, components of the weakened or killed viruses in vaccinations, or the needle or vaccine apparatus itself. Symptoms are also mysterious, seemingly disconnected, and cannot be treated or cured by medicine; medicines may be used to address and abate symptoms, but the nature of the injury is systemic and untreatable or incurable as a whole. So, in this example, the speaker references going to numerous doctors, many of whom can treat her symptoms but not cure her disease. Symptoms are also all-encompassing. They impact the person's livelihood and total well-being; she often notes that the contrast before and after is both physical and mental. So, in this case again, the speaker describes body pain as well as being unable to read a book. Afterwards, the speaker describes a life that is significantly diminished, where she cannot be a good mother because of the effects of the vaccine and how it has affected her life.

It is tempting to interpret before-and-after narratives such as this as a simple logical fallacy, specifically of the *post hoc ergo propter hoc* variety, or of confusing causation with correlation; Jacobson et al. might look at such a series of stories and experiences as confirmation bias or as one of a number of "flaws in reasoning." But rather, rhetorically they operate more powerfully than such conclusions indicate. As confessions, they assert the speaker's experience as true, as an embodied response to the exigence of injury. Similarly to Hall's cue card confessionals, the speakers use the confessional space to retell a narrative within their own terms, making the personal statement of injury a story retold not just in an effort to connect to others or build community (though some of these narratives undoubtedly do that) but also to serve a political function as present, material, evidentiary basis for injury as an exigence. As these stories proliferate across spaces online, they add arguments of quality to the public discourse on vaccination, demonstrating how serious and severe even risks that are deemed to be "rare" are (Lawrence "Fear"; Perelman and Olbrechts-Tyteca), but also work together to provide arguments of quantity. All together, these stories create a material rhetorical argument that vaccine risks are *not* rare, that these stories of injury *are* attributable to vaccines and not to a host of other conditions or unrelated phenomena, and that consequently risk calculi provided by experts in science and medicine are misguided. The confessional before-and-after form leverages the truth-making capacity of the individual story against the truth-making capacities of dominant discourses in science and medicine. Thus, to dismiss these arguments as flaws in thinking ignores how powerfully and persuasively they are able to respond to material exigencies in vaccination, as the narratives discussed below demonstrate as well.

Vaccine Injury Videos

YouTube videos that describe and document vaccine injury also offer potent examples of how parents reframe and reshape arguments about the safety of vaccines. These videos use photographic evidence to create montages of photos of a child with a variety of disabilities, conditions, or delays that are attributed to vaccine injury. Most of these videos feature young children and are posted by parents or grandparents, although some feature teenage girls who describe their own vaccine injury from Gardasil. Regardless of the nature of the injury or the specifics of the child's experience, the story told through the video is always one of loss, where the narrator of the video begins by having something—often a healthy baby who is a vibrant part of a functioning family—which is then lost, by the end of the video, through the vaccine. These videos use the structure of the before-and-after narrative, crafted through image and language use to reaffirm the validity of the subjects' experiences and to reinsert the particular, painful experiences of their children and families into discourses about vaccines.

Usually around four minutes long, the videos first feature happy, healthy, thriving children, and then a transition frame notes the first, or most troublesome, vaccine. After that, a slow (or sometimes drastic) digression of developmental capabilities is pictured. The videos typically show photographs that demonstrate declined interaction and mobility. They end with a black screen with some kind of expression of commitment to the child and a wish, hope, or prayer that the child "comes back" from the disorder. For example, in the instance of "Ana's Montage," the opening screen states that the video is a "tribute" to Ana in hopes that her "health will one day return," and the video ends with a screen that asks "May God guide you back to us." Throughout the video, the before-and-after story relates a narrative with hope of regaining this once "normal" child who has been lost through vaccines.

What's significant about this structure is the notion of loss and the impact on the family embedded in the "before and after" narrative. Most of these videos make a point of not only showing healthy children pre vaccine but showing healthy children who are well integrated into happy families. Early images tend to show healthy babies sitting with grandparents and playing with siblings; however, over the course of the before-and-after structure of the story, the child becomes increasingly detached—quite literally absent from the family. By structuring the story in such a way, the video amplifies the change that the vaccine injury causes the entire family, making not just the child suffering with the disability present but a network of parents, grandparents, brothers, and sisters who suffer as well. In this sense, the structure makes the child's absence rhetorically present through the course of the video as the child regresses from normal family activities.

The videos also show a few key images that serve some specific purposes in how the rhetoric of presence establishes injury. Many of these videos make a point of showing many of the developmental milestones that parents claim are proof that their children were developing normally before vaccines—eye contact, attention, standing, cruising, walking, playing, and manipulating objects. After the vaccine, the pictures also show a child who cannot stand easily, who appears distant or who does not make direct eye contact with the camera, and who simply looks ill, pale, or upset. Weight is also an important feature of the vaccine injury videos. Illnesses and disorders of the digestive tract (particularly severe diarrhea) are often associated with the onset of autistic symptoms following vaccination and are actually the source of the purported connection between autism and the MMR vaccine posited by the discredited Wakefield study. In this case, the pictures leading up to the transition frame show a healthy, almost chubby baby, but after the "Then one day, things started to change" frame comes an image of a visibly thin child, usually with a midsection that is concave. The captions also record digestive problems, with statements such as "Your body stopped metabolizing food," "And you became thinner and thinner," and "Your body became a battle ground, your digestion totally compromised." Other videos document other physical limitations, such as regression in motor functions or the ability to walk, always presented as the results of the vaccine injury. Many of the videos also contain language indicating that the parents see the child as "locked" inside his or her own body and that somehow they will eventually remedy the vaccine injury, and the whole child will be restored.

Videos and montages such as these take the physical bodies of children whose parents have determined that they have experienced a vaccine injury and display them in an effort to provide evidence of the perceived real, physical toll of vaccines on their children and families. The healthy child represents a "before" of an ideal, healthy child who is an active member of the family, and the injury is expressed as a loss of these qualities. Although the child is living and therefore not actually lost, loss of health, of vitality, of progression, and of family unity and happiness are described as resulting from the vaccine. Responding to the material exigencies of injury, the experiences of the child and the family are understood entirely through the lens of their child *being injured*; consequently, parent narrators often express guilt at having exposed their child to the risk of injury by having them vaccinated in the first place. Therefore, even though these particular before-and-after confessionals are not authored by the child, the speaker still uses this space not just to confess and share the intimate details of a difficult experience but also to attempt to assuage the guilt of being responsible for the loss that they are so acutely experiencing. Guilt over the risk of injury also motivates the parent to continue to "witness" or to tell the story so that others might have the information that they didn't have and instead choose to avoid the risk of vaccination.

NVIC Vaccine Memorial

Beyond these individual posts and sites, the National Vaccine Information Center (NVIC) hosts the "International Vaccine Memorial," which functions as a space for families to share stories of vaccine injuries. The NVIC was founded by Barbara Loe Fisher (quoted at the outset of this chapter and cofounder of the advocacy group DPT) and describes itself as "an independent clearinghouse for information on diseases and vaccine science, policy, law and the ethical principle of informed consent" (NVIC, "About"). Overall, the website functions to provide alternative information about vaccines and advocates for parent choice about vaccines under the auspices of informed consent guidelines.

The memorial is just one part of the site, which functions to collect and amplify claims of injury resulting from vaccination that are usually not validated through scientific or medical means. The Memorial page describes itself as "offer[ing] families around the world the opportunity to post stories and photos about what happened to their loved ones so that others can become educated about the signs and symptoms of vaccine reactions in order to prevent vaccine injuries and deaths" ("International"). Key to the expressed purpose of this part of the site is "Witnessing," offering the expressed purpose of collecting, materializing, and perpetuating the need for choice in the face of vaccine mandates, as the site goes on to say:

> Whether your adult son was injured by the DPT vaccine as a child, or your newborn died after getting seven vaccines on one day, or you became disabled after getting an anthrax vaccination as a soldier, or your grandmother was crippled by flu vaccine, this Memorial gives you the opportunity to witness for the world about your experience with vaccination. It gives you or a person you care about a voice so that, someday, others will have a choice. ("International")

The memorial functions as a space where the public can provide a range of arguments that counter the dominant message from medical, scientific, and public health experts that vaccines are safe because injuries from them are relatively rare. As the excerpt above also shows, this space reflects the diversity of experiences that are deemed "vaccine injuries," moving beyond claims about infant reactions, MMR and autism, and even Gardasil injuries to problems with vaccination through adulthood, indicating that injuries from vaccinations can happen to anyone, anytime, throughout the lifespan. Such a practice harkens back to Hall's confessionals, wherein witnessing is a key truth-making rhetorical tactic—it uses the communal spaces and participatory nature of the internet to invite the world to validate claims of injury and reify material exigencies.

As vaccine injury confessions, these texts collect, reify, and respond to the multitude of ways in which vaccine injuries occur while also validating the personal experience as a form of evidence in vaccine debates. More than just an appeal to pathos, or expression of logical fallacy, or confusion of causation and correlation, the stories establish the specific claim that these experiences are vaccine-induced injuries using rhetorics of presence and confession within

the before-and-after structure to validate their claims. Photographs of children meeting milestones or developing in healthy ways prior to vaccination
work directly to refute the scientific argument that pre-existing developmental
symptoms are simply detected after vaccination. The accompanying narration
tells the reader or the viewer that particular, individual experiences of their
children are relevant pieces of data in response to the exigency of injury. By
looking at vaccine injury confessionals all together as claims to the rhetorical
authority of firsthand experience over remote and objective scientific knowledge, we can see how these rhetorics in the debate are not just the discourses
of misinformed, misguided parents and patients but rather work to respond
to the exigence of injury in important, crucial ways that continue to fuel discord. As persuasive texts, these confessionals create the conditions for vaccine controversy and sustain notions that vaccines can cause harm well after
science and medicine have concluded that they are safe and effective ways to
prevent disease. Within a response to exigencies of injury, however, vaccination presents the risk—not the diseases it protects against. Such a situation is
particularly constraining as it encounters the other exigencies and discourses
responding to exigencies disease and eradication. With diseases as traceable,
scientifically verifiable risks to communities and injuries standing as uncertain collections of anecdotes and personal experiences, the potential for conflict, especially when those separate exigencies are neither comprehended nor
modified, is significant.

RHETORICAL AUTHORITY, RHETORICAL PRESENCE

For those convinced that vaccine injury is not only more prevalent but more
serious than medical authorities acknowledge, the material exigencies of injury
loom large. In a rhetorical situation where vaccination risks disease rather than
prevents it, vaccine refusal functions as a similar effort to control and contain
injury, coming (potentially) into direct conflict with the doctor's response to
disease or the public health practitioner's desire for control and eradication.
Within the exigence of injury, conceptualizing a child's illness as injury, locat-
ing the cause of the injury in the vaccination, and retelling the story to others as evidence of harm serves a secondary purpose to make these uncertain
conditions these children experience controllable and tangible. This strategy
offers an explanation, a reason for why the injury happened, and perhaps a
route to remedy. This is perhaps why vaccination controversy discourses are
so inflected with the epideictic on both sides—"vaccines are the savior of the
world" on the one hand and "vaccines killed my child" on the other. Vaccines function as medical technologies with incredible, yet invisible, power. In

medicine, they offer the power to control the spread of disease, arguably one of medicine's most fundamental preoccupations, and among some members of other publics, an incredible explanatory power in the face of rising cases of diseases with unknown origins.

Medical responses to vaccine skepticism typically implore parents to "know the facts" about vaccines, on the premise that, with scientific data, parents will be able to make good choices for their children (i.e., they will choose to vaccinate them) (Poland). However, when doctors in particular make that appeal to parents, they are also reifying their own forms and systems of knowledge, and most often their own sources of authority, which can be perceived as coming at the expense of the parents' knowledge and authority. This creates a problem of rhetorical authority as addressed by McGee and Lyne. They argue that "credible experts, on the rhetorical model of authority, must facilitate the act of judgment—that is, they must speak that language of knowledge which translates easily into the language of action and promotes a fusion of the two" (391). The doctor knows that most parents do not actually have access to hard scientific data or know how to use that data alone to make valid decisions. So when the doctor says "know the facts," she is in essence saying "since you can't really know the facts, just listen to me and do what I say." This is not an action of facilitating judgment as much as it is an action that denies the possibility of good personal judgment on the part of the audience.

Furthermore, issues of control and power influence the ethos of the doctor in this scientistic rhetoric. As McGee and Lyne state, "If the general public appears convinced that experts must play an important role in the political economy, it does not want them to control it" (389). As this observation indicates, an appeal to scientific expertise is not persuasive on the grounds of its expertise alone without additional public input. After all, we all know that "because I said so" is an expression of power more than of persuasion. Therefore, to contribute to ethos, the value of the speaker's expertise must seem relevant and be earned for it to become persuasive. However, a doctor's appeal to her own expertise in the "know the facts" rhetoric demonstrates both an invocation of the doctor's power and valuation of her expertise over the parent's, neither of which builds the doctor's ethos. Within McGee and Lyne's assessment, therefore, an appeal to "know the facts" is troublesome because it posits a situation where expertise alone has value in and control over the vaccine decision.

The doctor's rhetorical authority, grounded in his or her own scientific expertise, is generalized (since scientific knowledge is only sound when generalizable) and therefore unspecific to the child. Following McGee and Lyne's assessment, the appeal to science is "inactive" and does not facilitate specific decision-making; therefore, it can seem esoteric and indifferent to the pain and suffering of parents, families, and children. By contrast, the parent's source of authority is the concrete, suffering child who is present in and the subject of the personal story. By resorting to less accessible evidence and data for the doctor's arguments, the doctor's appeal to scientific fact diminishes her ethos for the parent, whose present child seems to offer a more valid form of data.

More importantly, however, exigencies of injury loom large, powerfully, and persuasively across the controversy, and arguments that rely on scientific authority as a means of persuasion in particular fail to comprehend and modify this exigence. Injury confessions, therefore, represent a powerful force that shapes what vaccines are and how they operate as public objects—they are not just inert scientific objects destined to prevent disease and eradicate it from the planet. They are also injurious objects that represent risk and harm in a wide range of ways. By validating the commonalities across lived experience, injury confessionals seek to inform novices about the dangers of vaccines and to establish communities among those who feel that their children have been injured. By addressing the exigence of injury, these online narratives also counter hegemonic discourses that fail to comprehend the exigencies offered by nondominant agents—offering evidence, in the form of their children, that makes claims not authorized by science. By using confessional rhetoric to counter medical conclusions about vaccinations, the writers of these narratives attempt to make truth claims regarding their experiences through the online format, leveraging the epistemological capacities of confession to validate these claims (Hall).

Both the telling and the reading of personal stories empower participants to value forms of knowledge that differ from those the doctor advocates, which patients may see as subject to biases that the doctor doesn't want to acknowledge, like the economic demands of the pharmaceutical industry. Access to other personal stories allows online participants to then make decisions according to a variety of perspectives and experiences, even if those decisions contradict the recommendations of a doctor. Finally, by choosing to value a source of nonhegemonic authority—like the injury narrative—online spaces are a site of agency for people who feel disempowered by the dominant values of biomedical discourse. Thus, parents who believe their children have been injured by vaccines (or patients who believe they are victims of injury themselves) build authority and truth as they respond to exigencies of injury online.

INJURY AND BEYOND: RISKING THE UNKNOWN

Understanding injury as exigence explains many of the varied and ever-changing discourses offered by parents to counter vaccination mandates: that "more science" is needed to prove that the quantities of aluminum (or formaldehyde or neomycin or calf cells) are safe, that crony capitalism or "the government" is shading physician opinions of vaccines, that the personal anecdotes about the friend-of-a-friend's child who was "brain damaged" after receiving a vaccine are valid rationales for refusing a vaccination, and so on. It's not just that parents don't understand statistical risk estimations or that doctors are too paternalistic to be open to parent agency. It is that the material exigence of injury fails to be modified by the discourses available to the physician or that a physician is simply not addressing the shared discursive environment, even though they may be sharing a physical one.

By widening the scope of understanding of how vaccines shape and change discourse, these findings demonstrate a possible explanation for discord that produces and facilitates vaccination controversy not produced by parental deficit and therefore offer important lessons for those hoping to intervene in vaccination controversy—and for RHM scholars in particular. Beyond specific forms of injuries from vaccinations, however, an additional set of discourses work to respond to the harms that could come with vaccination; these unknowns, the subject of the next chapter, function powerfully as material exigence to create particularly contentious rhetorics about the many and various, long-term and short-term, negative health consequences of vaccines.

CHAPTER 4

Persuasion and the Unknown

IF ANY specific vaccination invokes every facet of vaccination controversy yet also demonstrates how the issue defies easy solution, it is flu. Flu is a serious threat to the public's health, sickening and even killing thousands of people every year. Flu has a long history, most infamously the 1918 "Spanish Influenza," which caused an estimated 50 to 100 million fatalities worldwide (Barry). The specter of another pandemic with such widespread morbidity and mortality haunts contemporary responses to influenza outbreaks, motivating efforts, from public health policy to scientific research, to develop better vaccine technologies, as vaccines are perceived to be the best defense in the event of another pandemic. Flu is also unique in terms of how it operates as a virus and in its social and cultural meaning: (1) influenza viruses mutate so quickly that the human immune system can fail to recognize mutated influenza viruses from season to season; (2) flu viruses can cause a wide range of symptoms, from relatively mild to severe with little warning; (3) because it is a viral illness, few treatment options exist for even the most serious of cases; and (4) flu is often publicly perceived as a common illness from which there is little to no actual threat, especially to healthy people.

These complexities of the flu create confounding problems for the vaccine. The rapid mutation of influenza viruses requires annual vaccination throughout a person's lifetime. The quantity of strains means that no vaccine is perfect, and even someone who was vaccinated can still get the flu. Despite intensive international surveillance of flu and viral activity, pandemics can grow beyond health officials' ability to control swiftly. Although health authorities agree that flu vaccine is the best available option for responding to a pandemic if it were to occur, flu vaccine is also notoriously viewed with suspicion, and not just by hard-line "anti-vaxxers" or those with skepticisms typically associated with childhood vaccination. For example, health care workers, those with presumably high levels of scientific education and at the highest risk for contracting and spreading flu, are notoriously hesitant to vaccinate for a variety of reasons, including low levels of perceived risk, low levels of perceived efficacy of the vaccine, and concerns about side effects (Cortes-Penfield).

In this chapter, I argue that fears of vaccination operate as more than just a set of discourses that express worry or conspiracy theories among the public but rather reflect *the unknown* as a material exigence. The unknown is the complex of consequences that are unintended yet could happen as a result of vaccination. The unknown includes consequences that are specific and perhaps even scientifically disproven, like getting the flu from the flu vaccine, in addition to generalized, long-term consequences, like long-term damage to the immune system. Rhetorically, the unknown functions to shape and constrain discourse as material exigence, as the uncertainties of science are ontologized into real, embodied risk.

To understand this material exigence, this chapter examines material exigencies of flu vaccine as expressed in a study of adults conducted in April 2018 (IRB# 1198211-1). I use S. Scott Graham's notion of constitutive calibration (*Politics*) to analyze how the unknown is ontologized in vaccine discourse, arguing that these discourses calibrate arguments about the body, its operation, and the possibility of unknown consequences resulting from science and medicine into a material exigence in vaccination controversy. Across these complex, multifaceted discourses, the negotiation of material exigencies created by the flu vaccine constrain and shape each participant's relationship to the vaccine. Vaccinating and nonvaccinating participants alike described concerns surrounding the vaccine that were deeply embedded in the material, embodied experience of being vaccinated, of what the vaccine can do to the body, and of the unknown consequences of being vaccinated. Overall, I argue here that as these risks and uncertainties are ontologized, they express limits of medical regimes like vaccination, reflecting how material exigencies of vaccination operate to constrain discourse.

MATERIAL EXIGENCE: CALIBRATING
THE UNKNOWNS OF FLU

In 2010 the Centers for Disease Control and Prevention (CDC) changed its guidelines to recommend that all adults over the age of six months be vaccinated annually against the flu. This change in recommendation significantly expanded the coverage requirements for flu vaccine, which had previously only recommended that children, pregnant women, elderly people, and those with compromised or weakened immune systems get the shot. This change also ushered in a new regulatory premise for vaccinating all adults. Since 2010 moderate progress has been made in increasing adult vaccination rates, but overall, healthy adults vaccinate far less frequently than other groups (Hillson et al.). Some degree of adult nonvaccination results from convenience- and cost-related barriers that could be addressed by interventions like flu shot clinics in workplaces or free flu shots. However, such measures alone would not address significant, overwhelming concerns levied about flu vaccine that involve the interplay between the perceived entanglements of disease versus the risks of the vaccine, even among knowledgeable adult populations (Prematunge et al.; Nitsch-Osuch and Brydak).

Consequently, flu vaccine is incredibly fraught. Low levels of perceived public risk from flu combined with low levels of confidence in the vaccine's efficacy make achieving high levels of vaccination coverage—which is necessary for improving efficacy—a challenge. At the same time, there is no other case across vaccination in which persuasion is so necessary to ensuring high levels of vaccination and community-level disease prevention. Unlike vaccinations like MMR, Hib, or Gardasil, flu vaccines must be administered annually, meaning that they must be given to adults repeatedly in order for public health officials to achieve appropriate levels of community immunity and protection from disease. Because childhood vaccinations are tied to school entry, they are relatively easy to mandate, but few such mechanisms are available for adults, which essentially forecloses on the possibility of compulsion for vaccinating adults. In the case of expanding flu vaccine coverage, persuasion is an important avenue for getting adults to vaccinate.

Moreover, flu vaccine *is* risky. Suspicions about serious, life-altering side effects are not without precedent—the history of flu vaccine is marred by scientifically validated unexpected side effects and adverse events. Notable cases include Guillain–Barré syndrome resulting from the 1976 swine flu vaccine, which ultimately caused 450 cases of the disorder and fifty-three deaths

(Israeli et al.; Miller et al.; Principi and Esposito). In addition to this historical example, the 2009 H1N1 vaccine caused narcolepsy among children in Sweden and Finland. These cases were caused by Pandemrix, the flu vaccine used in Europe during the 2009/2010 H1N1 epidemic (WHO, "Statement on Narcolepsy"; CDC, "Narcolepsy Following"; Brown; Ahmed et al.; Vogel). The latter case here is interesting. The 2009/2010 H1N1 vaccine was widely criticized and rejected by many people, despite assurances among the scientific and public health establishments of the vaccine's safety. Although Pandemrix was not administered in the US, and no other flu vaccines have been proved to cause other serious conditions, this was precisely the concern that critics of the vaccine voiced in their objections to it: that some kind of unexpected consequence could result from accepting the vaccination. For vaccine skeptics in particular, such occurrences materialized long-suspected concerns about the risks and uncertain benefits of vaccines in general and flu vaccine in particular.

Risk and Uncertainty

Risk and uncertainty are an inherent part of medicine, science, and related public decision-making. Thus, understanding the rhetorical qualities and operations of these components of medicine and science is a long-standing concern of those in the rhetoric of science and medicine (Teston, *Bodies in Flux*; Walker; Walker and Walsh; Retzbach and Maier; Lehmkuhl and Peters; among many others). Doctors, public health officials, and other health care practitioners know this too—rare is the intervention, drug, or procedure that is without some kind of complicating result. From the "side effect" to the "adverse event," the connotation of the former as both mild and common while the latter as serious and therefore exceedingly rare, medicine often accepts and acknowledges these worries as a part of the art and science of medicine. Derrida called this *pharmakon*—the possibility of remedy and poison in one that we understand to be an inherent part of medicine. However, risk and uncertainty operate in different ways in vaccination, primarily because, for some, health is risked by vaccinating, not an outcome of vaccination (see chapter 3). Although we might accept the stomach ache that comes with taking an aspirin, we appreciate its ability to alleviate our headache more. But this is not the case with a vaccine. The achy arm, mild fever, or fatigue from the vaccine harms without any certain, immediate therapeutic value. The idea that someone would risk certain health over the uncertain possibility of illness changes the risk calculus around vaccination, particularly among those who are skeptical about the benefits of the vaccine.

Trying to craft persuasive messaging in response to this difficult context has long been a concern of public health. Standard public health approaches to vaccination—such as those guided by the health belief model—offer problematically linear conceptualizations of understandings of risks, benefits, and decision-making, which are part of the reason for the historic ineffectiveness of these messages in encouraging adult flu vaccination in particular. The health belief model was developed in the 1950s and 1960s by Irwin Rosenstock and public health researchers who wanted to understand why people chose not to participate in preventive public health measures, such as immunization (Rosenstock "Historical Origins" 328). Researchers hypothesized that individual "life spaces" were composed of things that were positively valued, negatively valued, and neutrally valued. As Rosenstock first theorized, "Diseases, if they were represented in the life space at all, would be regions of negative valence which could be expected to exert a force moving the person away from that region" (330). The resulting health belief model posits that three factors influence the amount of negative value that a disease has for a life space: perceived susceptibility, perceived seriousness, and perceived benefits of taking action. Meanwhile, three additional factors—perceived barriers, self-efficacy, and cues to action—create the conditions most likely to identify and produce the desired preventive health action (Kloeblen and Batish 328). Within this paradigm, susceptibility to and seriousness of disease are the primary conditions for producing negative valence and setting the stage for the desire for prevention. Therefore, assessing and responding to seriousness and susceptibility are vital components of predicting and interpreting health behavior under this model. The results of such analysis are evident in vaccine promotional efforts and even some news reporting, where serious, though exceedingly rare, complications of disease are highlighted as a rationale for getting a vaccination (Carroll). Amplifying the notion that diseases are riskier and more serious than we might assume them to be, the health belief model guides, will increase negative valence associated with disease and make individuals seek out prevention.

However, scholars have pointed out that assuming that disease is inherently risky and that avoiding it is inherently beneficial makes normative assumptions about an individual's desired natural state as disease-free (Hobson-West). By contrast, when someone is as familiar with a disease as many are with the flu, it may be perceived as a known, certain experience compared with an unknown, uncertain one of being vaccinated; beyond this, contracting disease may even be beneficial within this purview, giving the immune system an opportunity to improve or enhance by contracting disease (Lawrence, Hausman, Dannenberg; Hausman, "Immunity, Modernity").

[Conceptualizing vaccination decisions and resulting persuasive efforts as weighing the risks of disease versus benefits of preventing it relates to the certainty/uncertainty paradigm in science and medicine, as it assumes that (1) disease is a source of uncertainty that will be avoided, (2) uncertainties only come up as problems to be solved, and (3) uncertainties are temporary states that exist only until a piece of data is encountered that transforms uncertainty into certainty.] However, uncertainty is a necessary part of the scientific process and is therefore bound to scientific conclusions and discourse, a circumstance that is highlighted in vaccination controversy (Schwartzman et al.). From media reporting of scientific data, which configures messages to reflect a variety of agendas, audiences, and rhetorical purposes (Fahnestock, "Accommodating Science"), to the lack of consensus on scientific issues even among experts, lay understanding of science "signif[ies] to non-experts that risks remain unknown" (Schwartzman et al. 3). Furthermore, "scientific research seldom increases certainty . . . given the rate of change in science and technology" (4), leading Schwartzman, et al. to conclude that "risk calculi premised on discrete values may need to be replaced" and that resulting "data and recommendations will be profoundly affected by the rhetorics of uncertainty" (4). Similarly, Pru Hobson-West has argued that understanding vaccine decision-making through the lens of risks and benefits oversimplifies the field of contexts within which opinions and decisions about vaccines are made. Instead, Hobson-West advocates conceptualizing vaccination decisions as made among a field of uncertainties: "The concept of uncertainty could instead be used to admit 'unknowable unknowns'" (279). Hobson-West states, "In the debate over vaccination, however, we need reminding that risk is just one possible response to uncertainty, and is our attempt to place order on an uncertain world by making the 'incalculable calculable' (Beck 1994: p. 181)" (279). This perspective misunderstands the contexts within which vaccination decisions are made. Risks also presume a normative horizon of lost security: "Statements on hazards are never reducible to mere statements of fact. As part of their constitution, they contain both a theoretical and a normative component" (Beck 27). The evaluation of flu as serious presupposes not having the flu or wanting to avoid the flu as the normative response to perceived flu risk. However, if the subject believes that contracting a serious disease is actually beneficial to the body, then that subject's normative stance is not avoiding the flu, no matter how serious it is. By contrast, a state of uncertainty can exist as a complex of internally persuasive discourses emerging out of values, beliefs, and concerns. Some of these uncertainties may be perceived as risks, while others may be perceived as benefits, questions, or other preoccupations regarding the best way to retain personal health.

Calibrating the Unknown

S. Scott Graham's notion of constitutive calibration offers a useful paradigm for understanding how these risks and uncertainties associated with vaccination operate as material exigencies in vaccination controversy. For Graham, calibration is the reifying process by which phenomena, like disease or pain, are ontologized in medicine. Graham borrows the term from Annemarie Mol, who calls calibration an "adding up"—it is the process of gathering data points, including test results, imaging, and other assessments, that leads to diagnosis and confirmation of the presence of a disease or "reality" of a condition (87). In this process, sources of input also contribute their own epistemological values and weight; seeing the lump or the break or the nodule during the fMRI scan is more valuable than the subjective patient report of pain, for example. But the process of connecting the two (when they coincide) is constitutive calibration, which ontologizes, for Graham, pain.

A similar process is reflected in vaccination discourses that adults share about flu vaccine to ontologize vaccination risks and uncertainties into the unknown. Instead of "adding up" pieces of scientific evidence that are calibrated into a confirming diagnosis, as is the case with experts, this popular calibration adds up uncertainties and calibrates them into visceral, embodied risks of the unknown (Johnson "'A Man's Mouth'"). Popularly, publics calibrate to the unknown uncertainties across science and medicine: skepticisms about pharmaceutical companies and collusion with government officials to require vaccines for financial benefit, past vaccine skepticisms that were at first dismissed but then turned out to be true, and methods for interpreting the body and how it responds to the experience of being vaccinated are not disparate discourses simply levied when suitable. The unknown is real because uncertainty is a part of science and medicine; popular calibration defines and determines how these uncertainties come together to establish material exigencies that bound and constrain discourse, complicating vaccine rhetorics, allowing them to consist of scientifically validated concerns and consequences of flu vaccine as well as popular myths and concerns and alternative understandings of the body and how it responds to disease and medicine.

"The unknown" as material exigence is powerful. As a shifting set of embodied states of risk, the unknown is often configured as a future self who suffers some kind of negative long-term consequence from repeated exposure of the body to medical and scientific intervention. This state can also be extrapolated beyond the self, to family, community, and the world, whose health is jeopardized by widespread uptake of the flu. Such an exigence becomes doubly powerful when perceived to be an unknown consequence of science itself, something doctors and scientists either don't know about, haven't seen yet, or do know about but aren't disclosing. Overall, therefore, this material exigence shapes the operation of vaccination controversy writ large, as it engages questions about uncertainties of science, what it should be allowed to do to bodies, and what its limits are, since science ultimately is an enterprise of consequential unknowns.

Understanding how the unknown operates across flu discourse offers an opportunity to understand how such exigencies are responded to and articulated in the public sphere. In the interviews reported on here, vaccinating and nonvaccinating participants alike describe and configure risks, such as the risk of jeopardizing community health by not vaccinating and the risk of getting sick from the flu shot (or getting sick despite the flu shot) by vaccinating. However, in addition to these discussions and negotiations of risk, all participants directly or indirectly articulated looming, ongoing, unknown risks of what might happen after being vaccinated.

RISKING THE UNKNOWN: ADULTS AND FLU VACCINE

Of the thirteen people interviewed, six had gotten the flu vaccine and seven had not. As discussed later in this chapter, however, these choices were not necessarily indicative of vaccine support or detraction (some said they didn't want a vaccine but a job required it; others said they normally vaccinated but had forgotten); health over the winter months (in at least one case, a vaccinating interviewee contracted flu twice); or consistently positive or negative overall attitudes about the vaccine generally. Although all were college undergraduates, they represented a wide range of nontraditional ages (ranging from early twenties to mid-fifties), backgrounds (five reported either being from or spending extensive time in countries other than the US), and living situations (some lived in dorms with roommates, others at home with parents, and others in multigenerational homes with their own children). Thus, these interviews overall tell a diverse story about why people do and do not vaccinate, complicating easy answers about how to best prevent a disease like flu, persuade adults to vaccinate, or even begin eradication efforts when faced with such a ubiquitous disease.

To examine adult experiences and perspectives on vaccination, and flu and flu vaccine in particular, I conducted a small interview study of college students in spring 2018. Students were contacted through listserv messages and friend-of-a-friend referrals and were invited to participate in hour-long interviews with a faculty member and/or a team of graduate student researchers over Skype, by phone, or in person.[1] Interviews were conducted in a semi-structured format, where students were asked the questions in Table 3, but interviews were designed to be conversational, giving students space to openly discuss their experiences with and views on the vaccine.

In total, thirteen adults were interviewed over an approximately two-week period in the beginning of April 2018, which gave access to experiences with the most recent flu season, allowing us to ask them whether they got the flu or other serious illnesses during that season; how disruptive those illnesses were to their work, home, and school activities; and how the flu shot had factored in to their preventive health decisions that past year.

Transcribed interviews were then analyzed rhetorically, coding for arguments provided about the individual's decision to vaccinate or not vaccinate.[2] Three notable findings emerged. First, participants described an uncertain, indeterminate benefit of the vaccination itself; although some students said that they thought the vaccine was important, many equated getting the vaccine with other health behaviors, like eating organic, healthy food. Second, when risks are discussed, participants configure these as risks to their own bodies as well as to the public writ large, understanding things like trust in scientific and medical professionals as inherently risky. Third, some par-

---

1. For this work, I am indebted to my English 502 Research Methods in Professional Writing and Rhetoric seminar students who assisted with the conduct of these interviews: Brandon Cantrell, Luana Shafer, Kimberlyn Pepe, Emily Bourne, Manal Assad, Tara McVey, Jennifer Stevens, Paula Ferguson, Mae Bonem, Tamara Moorman, Stephanie Nelson, and Lauren Hoerath.

2. Breakdown of interview responses by flu shot decision are as follows:

Interview 1: Yes
Interview 2: Yes
Interview 3: No
Interview 4: No
Interview 5: No
Interview 6: No
Interview 7: No
Interview 8: Yes
Interview 9: Yes
Interview 10: No
Interview 11: Yes
Interview 12: Yes
Interview 13: No

TABLE 3. Flu study interview questions

WARM-UP QUESTIONS

1. Could you tell me a little bit about yourself? Where are you a student? What is your major, year, etc.?
2. Are you currently working? What do you do? How do you balance that with school?
3. Do you live on campus/off campus? With family, friends, a significant other?

EXPERIENCE WITH ILLNESS

1. Did you have the flu this year or last year? Or any other bad colds or respiratory illnesses?
   a. [If so] What was that like? Disruptive or not a big deal?
   b. [If not] Excellent! What did you do to stay healthy?
2. Would you say this was a typical experience for you this year?
3. Generally, how do illnesses like a cold or the flu impact your life? Do you miss work/school? Do you prefer to "tough it out"? Do you have a spouse, children, family members, or friends who are impacted?
4. Can you tell me about the worst cold or flu you've had? What happened? What made it so bad?

OPINIONS ON THE FLU SHOT

1. How does the flu shot factor into these experiences for you? Do you always get it/never get it?
   a. Why?
   b. How has that decision worked out for you?
2. How did you make the decision to get it/not get it this past year? What factors did you consider?
3. What do you think about the flu vaccine generally? Do you think it's important or necessary?
   a. Why / why not?
   b. Do you think it's more important for some people to get than others?
4. Do you remember hearing a lot about the vaccine—either this year or in the past?
   a. Why do you think people make a big deal about the vaccine?
   b. Where do you kind of put yourself in the issue—a bit supporter of the vaccine? Big detractor? Indifferent? Why?
5. Is there anything you think [your institution]—or other colleges—should be doing to try to keep students healthy during the winter months? What forms of support would you like to see universities offer to students who are ill with diseases like colds and the flu?

CLOSING

Are there are any other insights or opinions you'd like to share?

ticipants expressed generalized worries about the flu vaccine and its potential for negative health consequences, particularly through the articulation of widespread, unknown concerns about what the vaccine might do to an individual's or community's health over time. These were not characterized as "side effects" from flu vaccine, and they are not articulated as concerns about getting sick directly from the vaccine, like getting the flu from the flu shot, or even as injury. Rather, these concerns addressed what might happen to the body sometime after being vaccinated. Conceptualizing this range of risks and uncertainties as calibrated to material exigencies created by vaccinations—rather than disparate alternative theories or misunderstandings of science—offers an explanation for why these uncertainties remain so pervasive in vaccine discourse, opening up new opportunities for rhetorical response.

Why Adults Vaccinate

Unsurprisingly, those who were vaccinated tended to offer the most positive positions on flu and flu vaccine; however, such statements of support were not unilateral. Of the six vaccinating participants, two vaccinated for work-related reasons (one worked in a hospital that required the vaccine; the other began vaccinating when she worked as a caregiver for children). These latter two participants, though they ultimately vaccinated, primarily expressed reluctance and distrust of the vaccine even though they did get it. Such a phenomenon was not a part of this research but suggests the need for further study regarding the role that vaccine mandates play in increasing vaccine uptake while failing to abate concerns about the vaccine.

The remaining four vaccinating participants described a range of support for flu vaccine and vaccines in general, from unilateral strong support to ambivalence and neutrality on the need for the vaccine. Interviewees 9, 11, and 12 offered perhaps the strongest statements in support of the vaccine, describing it as beneficial to their health, easy to get, and something that everyone who can do, should do. Most significantly, two factors loomed largest in these decisions to vaccinate: being free of constraints like cost or convenience, and family influence on the decision.

The following excerpt reflects such a case as articulated by a vaccinating participant:

INTERVIEWEE: Like everyone in the house always got the flu vaccine. . . . And it was always just like oh, it's time to go . . . Like that yearly time to go get the flu shot.

INTERVIEWER: And generally, how is . . . How is always getting a flu shot worked out for you?

INTERVIEWEE: Always . . . It was just really convenient. Always, just that . . . Make an appointment. You just go. Or, even as I got older, and like didn't go to the pediatrician, I went to like the CVS and you could get a flu shot which is what I did last year. (Interview 11)

For this participant, flu vaccine is just something she always does, stemming from practices her family began when she was a child. Interestingly enough, this person described a range of serious respiratory illnesses during the previous flu season, even though she vaccinated. However, instead of functioning as a source of distrust or disappointment in the vaccine and its efficacy, the experience of these illnesses move the participant to blame herself for waiting too long to be vaccinated and therefore not being better protected earlier in the cold/flu season.

This perspective exists within a strong, larger opinion about the importance of vaccination, described in the excerpt below:

And reading more about like why people believe that, and because of [the Wakefield] study and all that, you know it's been disproven and all. So people believe that vaccines have an impact on children but, to me, it's . . . so disproven. So all these things . . . There's more things supporting that you should be vaccinated than um actual evidence supporting you shouldn't be vaccinated. And now you see all these kids coming with measles and mumps and stuff like that. And like these are illnesses that were proven as like years ago like a dark age to be extinct in the sense that people weren't getting them anymore. But now kids are getting them again, because they're not vaccinated. (Interview 11)

Here, in addition to describing general vaccine support, other material exigencies of vaccination are being responded to as well, specifically disease and eradication. This topic comes up in another articulation of vaccine support, by another participant who states in response to the question "Do you think it's more important for some people to get than others?": "No, I don't think anyone's off the hook. Again, like I think it's herd immunity type thing, like we're all stronger if we all are protected, you know?" (Interview 12). This participant, who has a sibling with serious medical problems, also describes getting the flu shot as an annual family practice, which continued for all of her siblings into adulthood. For these participants, the flu shot is the norm for themselves and should be the norm for everyone, responding to other material exigencies in vaccination.

Uncertain Benefits

Among participants who expressed skepticism about the vaccine or who did not vaccinate, vaccines were associated with a range of uncertainties and risks, from benign but consequential to serious. One consistent expression of uncertainty across skeptical discourses questioned the benefit of the flu vaccine, particularly in concert with other practices that could provide more certain benefit to health.

The following exchange offers an example of such an articulation:

INTERVIEWER: Do you, um, do you get your flu shot every year?

INTERVIEWEE: No, actually, I only get it when it's required from work or school. So (laughs) I never go out of my way.

INTERVIEWER: You never go out of your way to get it.

INTERVIEWEE: Yeah, to like go get a flu shot. So like, when I started this new job, I was asked to get a flu shot and then when I started [school], I was asked to do all of my, um, immune shots and stuff. Like, I never go out of my own way to do it which is really bad. (Laughs).

INTERVIEWER: (Laughs). Why do you think you don't go out of your way to do it?

INTERVIEWEE: I don't know. It's just, in a way I don't believe it. Like, being from a different country.

INTERVIEWER: Oh?

INTERVIEWEE: You know? Like I understand like germs do fly and stuff, but I just feel like what's meant to happen to me is gonna happen to me so I might as well just keep on pushing (Laughs). . . . And then with no health insurance, I think that's one of the reasons why.

INTERVIEWER: Sure.

INTERVIEWEE: With no health insurance, I don't even like think about doctors as a source. (Interview 2)

So here, this participant describes a set of conflicts regarding getting the flu shot—she will get it if it is required, but she doesn't think it's helpful, necessary, or accessible to her. The reasons for not getting the flu shot vary, from not having the financial means to afford it to the participant saying "I don't believe it" and that "what's meant to happen to me is gonna happen to me." Later in the interview, she elaborates by describing what she does when she gets sick: "With no insurance, I don't do any doctors 'cause just talking to them is already $160. . . . But I just take like homemade herbs and stuff and my mom's tea—favorite tea." For this student, although she might know that getting the flu shot is a good thing that she is supposed to do to prevent the flu, the situation is nevertheless laden with conflicts—costs are a big part of this, yes, but also what she describes as cultural and familial perspectives and practices, like drinking her mom's favorite tea and being from a different country as a reason that her perspective might be different. She caveats all of this by stating that "I understand like germs do fly and stuff." For this student, this comment is clearly important to make—she understands science, which is important to her as a social work student who works in a hospital, but she also has other beliefs that inform her views on flu vaccine more.

The uncertainties here are not necessarily about harm from the vaccine but about the good it could possibly do. If "what's meant to happen to me is gonna happen to me," then the vaccine is an addition to her practices that is costly financially while offering uncertain benefit, since she may get the flu even if she gets the vaccine. Overall, she simply thinks that there are other, better ways of preventing the flu than getting the flu shot. Such perspectives on the uncertain benefit that the flu shot offers, compared with other methods of disease prevention, were echoed in other interviews. Interviewees either who did not vaccinate or who expressed skepticism about the vaccine were far more likely to cite alternative ways of preventing illness as being just as good or more effective at preventing flu. These participants cited vegan and vegetarian diets (Interview 10), organic food (Interview 13), and dirt / getting sick (Interview 7) as sources of health that were preferable to the flu vaccine.

Other interviewees offered specific articulations of risks in getting the flu shot alongside these uncertain benefits. As one participant stated, "I have, I'm trying to remember when. I think it, when I was a rising junior, was when I had the flu shot. And then I had—I had a reaction to it. I don't know, I just like felt sick right after" (Interview 4). She also goes on to describe that she doesn't think that the flu shot is necessary:

INTERVIEWER: Do you think it's important, or necessary?
INTERVIEWEE: I mean, I don't think it's that necessary, because on the floor
    I live on, literally half the people had the flu, but then I didn't have my

shot. And, I was like interacting with them and everything, and I just
never got it, so.

INTERVIEWER: Do you know if they got the shot?

INTERVIEWEE: That's a good question. I know one of them did, and then
she ended up getting the flu, which is weird, but I don't know if the rest
did. But, I know this one particular girl, she did.

In this case, some people were vaccinated and others were not, yet the flu
seemed to strike indiscriminately among vaccinators and nonvaccinators
alike, and she never got sick. A student who plans to be a pediatrician, comes
from a family of doctors and scientists, and participates in the university's
model World Health Organization (WHO) is not a student indifferent to the
qualities of science or the importance of vaccination. But she sees no benefit
here, along with mild discomfort associated with getting the vaccine, which
together lead her to decide not to vaccinate.

Uncertain benefit is an important point of calibration across this material
exigence, because the flu vaccine *does* carry uncertain benefit to the individual. During the 2017–18 flu season, CDC's interim estimate of vaccine effectiveness was 36 percent, which was much higher than in recent years, which
saw efficacy rates of around only 20 percent (Flannery). Vaccine efficacy
rates vary from season to season, across age groups, and arising from which
strains are chosen to be included in the vaccine (Bonomo and Deem). Additional variables, like the robustness of an individual's response to the vaccine,
can also shape whether the vaccine will be effective at preventing the flu
or not. Hence, the uncertainty surrounding flu vaccine stems not only from
the uncertainty of risks associated with the vaccine but also from its overall
effectiveness at preventing illness. To be clear—flu vaccine is still important.
Even a 20 percent efficacy rate means a significant reduction in the number
of cases of flu, the robustness of circulating strains, and the seriousness of
complications from flu. But at the level of the individual, benefit is often less
certain.

Unknown Risks

Three participants in particular offered extended discussions or descriptions
of their concerns about flu vaccine outside of established concerns, like fear of
needles or getting the flu from the vaccine. That is, they articulated unknown
risks associated with getting the flu shot. Again, the unknown risk had a wide

range of rationales, like those about the financial incentives for mandating flu vaccine:

> Yeah, cause, like, um, I don't know. It's weird because I saw something about this—I don't know what—it was a city or a state—that they made it a requirement for kids to get vaccines and people were against it because it should be, like, their choices as parents if they want to get vaccines. So, I think, like that, they might require in the future you have to get a flu shot. So, that's why, and it might be the business they're getting off flu shots. So, that's why I think it's a money thing. (Interview 10)

Here, the risk calculus lies not in the benefits of the vaccine versus the risks of the disease but rather in the risks inherent in the larger apparatus that requires and produces vaccines. Again, this risk is accepted as part of our medical, scientific, and policy processes associated with developing and mandating vaccination: whether parental choice should or should not play in that process (and risk low rates of vaccination or the eliding of personal freedoms), the extent of the influence that money has on science, and the incentives that do or should exist across those who research and make vaccines and those who mandate them. The participant doesn't quite know what the connections are—making this comment overall a reaction to the unknown associated with science, medicines, and vaccines—but posits that the possibility is a rationale on its own for enduring skepticism.

Other participants expressed unknown, embodied risks of vaccinations, which primarily configured the site of vaccine risk as an uncertain, long-term harm likely to be experienced by the body. For these participants, risks associated with flu vaccination range from articulations about medicine not being good for the body generally, to specific concerns about what the vaccine could do to the body, to descriptions of damage to health caused by flu and flu vaccination. As one participant states:

> I just feel like the flu shot, vaccines, and all that stuff—I don't [think] they're good for your body. Just cause, I don't know. I'm more organic. I don't really like to take any pills or medications or any shots that are not necessary. So, I feel like I, I can prevent the flu. And if I do get it, like, a lot, maybe I'll get it then. But, other than that, I don't think I need any extra stuff in my body. (Interview 10)

This participant goes on to say that she doesn't take pain relievers or antibiotics either, because these things interfere with the body's natural mechanisms for healing. She describes teas, herbs, and other home remedies (like drinking warm milk mixed with garlic) as being more appropriate for restoring health. She concludes by saying, "No. Yeah, it's—and I think it's all of Bolivia—like most of the country is more organic. You drink, um, teas. You drink a specific—there's an apple tea, like, that you drink, and whenever I drink it I feel better, so. (chuckles) I don't know" (Interview 10). So, for this participant, there are specific risks associated with medicines as a method for retaining health, and (largely Western) interventions like antibiotics, pain relievers, or vaccines are seen as damaging and a greater source of risk than the illness, ailment, or alternative treatments that her parents and other cultures offer.

Two other participants offered different types of risk theories associated with vaccination. One participant's story goes as follows:

> INTERVIEWEE: In general, um, I, I, I thought that [the flu shot is] really not necessary. That's what I used to think, but, you know, 'cause I was working with uh, kids. I have to take it. But if I was never going to work with kids, I was never gonna take the flu shot, 'cause I'm like, "Why would they bring some . . . virus into my body?" (laughs) You know. Like, I'm not feeling sick, then they, they give you that virus. Then you feel a little sick after you take it.
>
> *Boundaries*
>
> INTERVIEWER: So do you believe that the flu shot causes illness?
>
> INTERVIEWEE: No, no, it, I think so in later. That's what I think.
>
> INTERVIEWER: Okay.
>
> INTERVIEWEE: Like, they, the way they, they put it is more like they say it will prevent the illness, right? But you're not going to know each year we have a different, you know, kind of . . . um . . . how could I put a right word for it? Um . . .
>
> INTERVIEWER: Like a strain?
>
> INTERVIEWEE: Yeah, like a strain. Like, it's a different strain that comes each year, right? So, if you, if, if they're going to be injecting you with all that different strains every year, there'll be one day when something will be triggered. That's what I think. That's my opinion. (Interview 9)

This interviewee begins by talking about typical side effects from getting the vaccine, such as getting the flu from the flu shot or feeling ill after the shot, the former of which is not scientifically validated whereas the latter is. However, when asked for more information by the interviewer, the participant elaborates that her theory is different from that and that the effects are farther-reaching than just feeling ill after the shot—that "there'll be one day when something is triggered." What that "something" is remains unclear in the interviewee's response (and perhaps even to the speaker), but such imprecision indicates how powerful the unknown is in shaping relationships to and interpretations of the disease. Something being triggered could be almost anything—an autoimmune disorder that is diagnosed years from now, a string of serious colds and flus that resist medical intervention because of a weakened immune system, even musculoskeletal problems that develop in the upper arm could be attributed to repeated jabs from the needle. The source and manifestation of the triggering are all undetermined, yet the risk is still articulated as real.

A similar theory was offered by Interviewee 7. A veteran and father of three children, this interviewee described many cases of intense illness as well as multiple experiences of vaccination during his military tenure. While he was in the military, he had to get annual flu vaccines at the same time every year, which he felt damaged his overall health over the long term. He stated at the end of the interview that he wanted to participate in the study so that he could share the following:

> INTERVIEWEE: The main thing I wanted to share with you it's the fact that I, I would get sick when I would get that shot around that time.
> INTERVIEWER: Yeah. So you mean that you would get the shot and then you would feel like you would get sick?
> INTERVIEWEE: Uh, no. Like I would stop taking the shot, and I would kinda get sick, want to get sick around that year. The next year around that I didn't get the shot.
> INTERVIEWER: I wonder why that . . . And you feel like that's happened a couple—
> INTERVIEWEE: A couple times yeah. But now it's gotten to a point where it's kinda like just it's more random where it tries to get me sick but I'm good. (Interview 7)

In both these theories, the long-term effects of the flu shot are described as actively damaging the body, actually lowering its resistance to the flu over time and, in a sense, forcing the participant to continue to vaccinate because of this weakness. In the case of Interviewee 9, she concludes that she has to keep getting the vaccine to avoid getting sick, whereas Interviewee 7 configures the flu as an active agent, trying to get him sick. Neither participant has a clear, specific theory about why or how this happens—there is just some kind of unknown damage that happens to the body that isn't experienced until well after the vaccine is administered.

The three participants who offered the most specific articulations of risks associated with vaccination shared some additional similarities—all three were originally from or lived for an extended period of time in other countries (Ghana, Guatemala, Bolivia); all three reflected on the differences between the US and these countries regarding health and flu-prevention practices, even though the interview questions did not specifically ask for that information; and all had unique concerns about what vaccines were doing to their bodies outside of what was being expressed or advertised to them. In particular, these participants commented on how other countries had different values or cultures around health, talking about healthy food and dirt and the value of those things for producing general health over techno-scientific interventions like vaccinations.

Across the interviews that expressed skepticisms about the vaccine, articulations of uncertainties and of risks are calibrated into an amorphous yet powerful unknown as the source of skepticism and exigence to which participants were responding to in their decision to not vaccinate. Distinct from other exigencies that coincide with skeptical attitudes about vaccination—like that of injury—the unknown is risk and uncertainty, embodied and functioning as material exigence that motivates discord. The responses of these participants not only demonstrate how powerfully the unknown operates across vaccination controversy but also highlight one of the most significant difficulties associated with existing persuasive tactics in response to vaccination skepticism.

RHETORIC AMID THE UNKNOWN

Although small, this study offers a range of positions on vaccines as maintained by adults. Nearly every participant had a varying degree of support and skepticism associated with flu vaccine, all produced a wide range of arguments about their decisions, and every participant offered different personal, often familial reasons for choosing to vaccinate or not. Obtaining such diversity in responses was not an explicit goal of the study. When beginning the interview, I did not know the participant's vaccination status, and, in fact, given that recruitment materials were sent to students with majors and interests in health in particular, as the list of interviewees grew, I anticipated more positivity all around—more vaccinators, more supporters of vaccination, more pro-science/anti-antivaccine discussion. But, as qualitative studies often do, the data didn't bear out my expectations at all.

As is also the case with qualitative research, though, the surprises are more instructive than the expected. The adults interviewed were all pursuing higher education, and many were nearly finished with their studies. Many were in science fields and pursuing careers in science. Yet, only four were motivated to vaccinate or even expressed significant, consistent forms of support for the vaccine. The remaining nonvaccinators or skeptics had some overlap in rationale—particularly around family influence and food and organic lifestyles—but otherwise had a wide range of reasons for not vaccinating. This range cannot be resolved through the mundane and easy-to-address public health intervention (like removing cost and convenience barriers by putting a free flu shot clinic on campus) or mandates alone. Even a free, mandatory vaccine was not enough to satisfy the skepticisms of one of the participants.

One of the biggest problems with current public health approaches to flu vaccine and understanding skepticisms about it, as Hobson-West also points out, is that it begins with deficit; its genesis starts with a program and looks at commonalities among people who did not participate in the program as a starting point. It looks at healthy people and assumes that their inherent, desired normality is health and that health is defined by absence of disease. It is logical within this paradigm to think that enhancing and emphasizing the public's sense of severity of disease will motivate vaccination; hence public health and communication objectives to try to amplify disease risks. By privileging lack of disease and stigmatizing nonvaccination, researchers lose rhetorical insight into how individuals weigh all the many varied uncertainties and risks created by vaccines. As these discourses show, people are responding to more than just the certainties of vaccination against the uncertainties of disease; they are responding to a much larger set of uncertainties and risks in science and medicine. The rhetorical approach advocated here—understanding these discourses as calibrated into material exigence—elucidates understanding of the issue in ways that other approaches have not.

Viewing concerns surrounding flu vaccination as responding to material exigencies of the unknown created by vaccines—rather than as deficits in understanding—reveals how skepticisms levied at vaccination are actually not as illogical, incoherent, or ignorant of science or risk statistics as they might seem at first glance. The unknown is actually a way of accepting, contending with, and responding to science, which ultimately comes with many uncertainties and risks that publics must choose to accept or reject. In a context of uncertainty, we can see how patients may perceive disease as certainty, not uncertainty, so choosing disease is actually a process of choosing a certain course of action rather than the uncertain process of vaccinating. Drinking garlic steeped in warm milk might be far more certain since, at the very least, it is a routine part of life practiced frequently by all members of the family, as opposed to the uncertain benefits of vaccination to the individual, which may or may not actually do anything to prevent flu. The risks inherent in being vaccinated—driving to a place to be vaccinated, risking even a mild side effect, accepting and trusting medical officials to have licensed and approved a safe vaccine—become real imperfections to which one must respond when seen as material exigencies. Even questions about the body and what the long-term effects of medicines might have on it become factors to contend with, unknowns that must be responded to. Every potential or perceived uncertainty or risk is made real and seeks modification, when understanding the unknown as a material exigence.

In this case, the unknown as material exigence offers one way of understanding how the complexities of uncertainties about vaccination work in terms of discourse yet also highlight the need for them to be acknowledged and addressed through rhetoric. Dismissing an adult's claim of uncertainty—even if it is expressed through an unlikely theory about the flu vaccine actually making someone's body more susceptible to the flu—as merely stupid or ignorant or based on an inaccurate understanding of science doesn't resolve the exigence or address the imperfection. Understanding the nature of the imperfection requires different methods of discourse to unpack and understand if resolution through persuasive means is to be sought. Otherwise, the only option that remains available to ensuring vaccination under such circumstances is compulsion.

ADDRESSING MATERIAL EXIGENCIES

The findings across *Vaccine Rhetorics* offer a variety of explanations for discord created by vaccines. This book argues that vaccines have always been and continue to be sites of controversy and disagreement because they are shaped and bound by material exigencies that constrain discourse and the persuasive options that discourse might attempt to make. For researchers in RHM, material exigence offers a way to understand the intractable and material qualities of debates involving health, medicine, and science.

The case of adult vaccination and the material exigence of the unknown offers an important insight into why vaccines are so controversial yet also demonstrates how new methods for communication, discursive intervention, and research in rhetoric are required if scholars in RHM are going to illuminate and intervene in such intractable public problems. As the final chapter of this book fully discusses next, modifying material exigence requires unique methods for problem-solving and persuasion. In the case of vaccination controversy, such an intervention might include reviving tried-and-true rhetorical practices like audience analysis alongside incorporating stakeholders into problem-solving efforts and re-examining how and where deliberative forms of rhetoric can illuminate the issue and restore some of its rhetoricity. Material exigence offers rhetoricians a new way of understanding public problems, and rhetorical methods are one possible way to transform that understanding into action.

Rhetorically Informed Persuasion and a Material Rhetorical Approach to Controversy in Science and Medicine

VACCINES ARE complex and multifaceted objects. They represent a long history of scientific achievement, understanding about disease, and advancements in medical practices and values. Yet, as this book argues, vaccination also inaugurates a set of key material exigencies, created by the vaccine as an object, that have caused particularly intractable forms of discord since the beginning of the practice. Disease, eradication, injury, and the unknown continue to constrain the rhetorics we use to discuss vaccinations, making calls for compulsion seem preferable to persuasion, obscuring possibilities for persuasive paths forward.

Vaccine Rhetorics charts why persuasion has become so difficult through the concept of *material exigence*—an imperfection, marked by urgency, created by the material operation of vaccines. In vaccination controversy, persuasion has become particularly difficult because key components of the rhetorical situation have not been understood: few people fully comprehend all exigencies, meaning that there can be no possibility for modifying exigencies that are not comprehended; these exigencies risk irrevocable material consequences that heighten urgency and contribute to discord; and reliance on deficit as an explanation for difference forecloses opportunities for productive rhetorical spaces and options to open. Consequently, compulsion seems like an advantageous, even more ethically responsible,[1] response to skepticisms about vaccines.[2]

Yet in light of such a conclusion, the evidence and arguments presented across this book articulate a rationale for retaining persuasion, arguing that the persuasive contexts where vaccines are discussed are constrained by material exigencies that complicate discourse and facilitate discord. Retaining the persuasive approach requires more than just maintaining the opportunity to persuade people to vaccinate; rather, *rhetorically informed persuasion requires making space for dissent, opportunities for deliberation, and mitigating exigencies that shape debate.* Such an approach challenges researchers, the public, and scientific and medical experts alike to acknowledge, embrace, and understand how vaccination is an evolving social, cultural, and embodied experience.

Books on vaccine controversy often conclude with a series of arguments, counterarguments, or considerations that researchers, health officials, practitioners, and the public might take on in order to better address concerns

---

1. These findings combine with perspectives from popular and scholarly researchers in ethics (Caplan, "Revoke," "Ethicist"; Constable et al.; Schwartz and Caplan), medical policy and ethics (Bayefsky; Looper et al.), and increasingly strong statements in favor of expanded mandates across professional organizations and publications (AAP, Omer et al.) that point to a desire for new regulatory approaches to vaccine hesitancy. Although some research still retains a stance focused on understanding and decision-making (Corben; Hendrix et al.), support for compulsion still reigns. Even in my home state of Virginia, in January 2016, Eileen Filler-Corn proposed HB 1342, which proposed to remove all nonmedical exemptions in Virginia (Virginia retains religious as well as medical reasons for exemptions to vaccination) (LIS > HB1342). Although this measure was swiftly rejected, as the successes of California's new exemption laws come to fruition, it is likely a measure that will be considered by other states as well.

2. Studies like those of Opel et al. and Nyhan et al. offer some of the best examples of the ways in which research conclusions are increasingly straying from persuasion. Opel et al. find that more forceful/less collaborative approaches to vaccine conversations are actually more effective at increasing rates of vaccination; participants in Opel's study who began the vaccine conversation with "so, we are going to get some shots today" rather than "what questions do you have about the vaccinations you will get today?" were more likely to administer a vaccination. Nyhan et al. tested a series of interventions on survey participants to see whether messages that increase "scientific correction" could increase likelihood of vaccinating. This study found that all these messages failed to increase reported likelihood of vaccinating among parents who expressed existing hesitation, and some actually decreased reported likelihood of vaccinating in the future in some cases. These findings were partially confirmed in Reavis et al. as well, who tested the concept in a similar study with similar findings. However, other researchers, such as Haglin, have not been able to reproduce Nyhan's "backfire effect" (Haglin). This "backfire effect" was picked up across media, however, and even popularly by Nyhan himself, as an argument for why interventions that rely on patient choice are ineffective because educating people about science can be so imprecise (Nyhan; Collins; Mooney).

about vaccines. This book does not do that. Such an outcome is contrary to the objectives of rhetoric. Rhetoric, as quoted by Aristotle at the beginning of this book, challenges us to see the available means of persuasion in any situation. This means that the analysis of vaccine discourses presented here does not neatly lead to a series of counterarguments that might be applied at will to convince hesitant parents to vaccinate or to persuade the public of a new vaccine campaign. Rather, I argue that this issue, and other large controversies involving medicine and science, requires a new approach entirely, a new lens for *seeing* what avenues of persuasion might look like: a *material rhetorical approach* to controversy in science and medicine (Clary-Lemon, "Archival"; Lawrence, "When Patients").[3]

In this concluding chapter, therefore, I first synthesize the arguments this book makes about material exigence, the value of a material rhetorical approach, and what new forms of knowledge it might produce. A material rhetorical approach connects the analysis of material exigencies to practices that might be adopted in research, intervention, and advocacy by researchers in rhetoric of health and medicine (RHM) and related disciplines. Analysis of material exigencies alerts the researcher to the ways in which material operations of key objects in controversy constrain rhetoric and possibly produce discord.

Then, I outline how this lens is useful to scholars in rhetoric and scholarship in RHM in particular. Retaining persuasion is important not only in the case of vaccine controversy but for other controversies in the public sphere that question the power that science and medicine should have in a democracy. I argue that such controversies make rhetorically informed persuasion even more critical to ensuring that public voices are heard, various forms of knowledge-making are acknowledged, and the opportunity for public decision-making is retained. By attending to these new parameters and requirements of rhetorical situations, scholars in RHM can, through our own analysis, scholarship, and outreach, offer new paradigms for intervention.

Finally, rather than recommend a series of finite discourses that one "side" of vaccination debate might deploy to convince the "other," this analysis ends

---

3. This concept builds on the theories of materiality discussed throughout this book and specifically uses the term *material rhetorical approach* used in Jennifer Clary-Lemon's 2014 "Archival Research Processes: A Case for Material Methods." Although the terms are the same, Clary-Lemon's concept of this approach offers a set of outcomes distinct from the analytical frame described here, since her work is more specifically focused on building theory of materiality for archival methods and methodologies. I also pick up this idea in my 2018 article "When Patients Question Vaccines: Considering Vaccine Communication through a Material Rhetorical Approach," which serves as the kernel of the ideas and conclusions presented here.

with theories, methods, and frameworks specific to the issue of vaccination controversy for producing rhetorically informed persuasion. The hope is that these suggestions might be taken up by researchers in RHM and related fields to enrich our perspectives on vaccination discourse in the public sphere.

THE MATERIAL RHETORICAL APPROACH

What does it mean to adopt a material rhetorical approach to public controversies involving science and medicine? Critically, this approach connects theory, analysis, and practice to lead to rhetorically informed persuasion in the following ways.

Understanding material exigencies. Material exigence is a way of acknowledging the components of scientific understanding that are real, that create and constrain discourse, and that perpetuate controversy. Instead of viewing arguments and counterarguments about vaccination as simply the biggest misnomers, inaccuracies, prejudices, or blind spots that various actors hold across a contentious issue, understanding material exigencies makes the operations of material objects knowable, revealing the "imperfections marked by urgency" of the rhetorical situation and making them open to modification.

Such a perspective shows how discourse produced about medicine—particularly discordant discourse—is more than just "anti" or denialist but is rather a particular way of responding to the material exigencies that phenomena related to health and medicine create. It's a materialist way of conceptualizing perceptions of risks and benefits, safety and harm, and the very nature of health itself amid controversial situations. If we think of these issues as a series of material enactments of the body, rather than as social constructs or ways of subscribing or not subscribing to the hegemony of science or simple right and wrong, rhetoricians can respond to the call for nuanced methods of research, engagement, and intervention anew, broadly acknowledging the multiplicities of realities that are created by medical interventions.

New discursive responses. Understanding the material exigencies of controversial issues can reveal the spaces that will be most difficult to modify by discourse alone. Skeptical parents will not be able to convince provaccine doctors that there is no value in eradicating measles. Pro- and antivaccine parents will never find common ground over whether Gardasil is completely safe, effective, and necessary. Mandating the flu vaccine didn't resolve concerns about its long-term effects for one of the participants in the flu study in chapter 4. Such arguments would have to respond to the nature of the vaccine's operation as an object itself. To try to modify its very nature as an object through discourse is to take on a challenging rhetorical task that, at least as far as vaccination controversy is concerned, has not historically been a successful persuasive tactic.

Spaces for persuasion. Given the constraints on discourse when modifying material exigencies, spaces where deliberative, rather than epideictic, rhetoric can be exchanged about controversial issues could offer better answers to large, intractable controversy. Vaccination discourse is already embattled in the spaces discussed in this book—the examination room, the media, parts of the internet, and some workplaces. Devising rhetorical strategies and tactics that are more sensitive and responsive to material exigence in these spaces is certainly one mechanism for reconsidering rhetoric and persuasion. But with a controversy involving material exigence, perhaps changing the material conditions of the rhetorical situation itself must be part of any persuasive solution. In such a case, convening new spaces where vaccinations can be discussed in a less contentious way, and opening those spaces to true deliberation, offers a more distributed approach to discussing contentious issues.

In the case of the work of *Vaccine Rhetorics,* such an approach leads to new possibilities for study and intervention in vaccination controversy, which the next section describes.

MATERIAL RHETORICAL APPROACH AND RHM

Throughout this text, I use a wide range of paradigms and concepts from rhetorical studies to unpack and explain the rhetorics of vaccination, using theories of materiality and ontology (Mol; Graham), medico-legal rhetorics (Schuster et al.; Grant, Reed, and Lawrence), and rhetorical presence and confession (McGee and Lyne; Perelman and Olbrechts-Tyteca; Hall) to analyze how various publics and public issues respond to the material exigencies of vaccination. In addition, the work of these and other scholars in rhetoric (Christa Teston's work on materiality, Scot Barnett and Casey Boyle's on rhetorical ontology, Jenell Johnson's notion of the visceral public, and Catherine Gouge and John Jones's work in wearable rhetorics, to name just a few) offers important perspectives on and theories through which the materiality of medicine might be more directly engaged and understood in different contexts and controversies in science and medicine.

The material rhetorical approach enabled by a study of material exigence can be particularly useful to scholars in RHM because it operationalizes analyses when examining and intervening in public controversies involving science and medicine by accounting for the constraints that matter places on discourse. Such an approach allows scholars in RHM to engage some of its core objectives; Amy Reed articulates these objectives in her 2018 bibliography of research in RHM as "examin[ing] language about health and medicine as produced by rhetors with limited agency; used by particular audiences, who may or may not share the intentions, values, beliefs, or practices of the rhetor; and reflecting and constituting ideology" (191). Such objectives are similarly described by Lisa Melonçon and J. Blake Scott in their editors' introduction to the journal *Rhetoric of Health and Medicine (RHM)*, where they outline the forms of scholarship and objectives of the work in *RHM*, including

1. "inform[ing] and ameliorat[ing] a particular set of health-related practices that privilege some stakeholders' expertise at the expense of others"; (v)
2. "[using and developing] hybrid rhetorical theories and analytic approaches that draw on other scholarly traditions, especially ones that theorize the relationship of rhetoric to materiality, subjectification, and culture"; and (vi–vii)
3. "challeng[ing] popular, medical, and academic assumptions about how to empower patients or health consumers, for example, and offer[ing] more nuanced ways to respect distributed expertise in health and medical contexts." (vii)

Across these descriptions emerges a set of central charges that work in RHM can do: challenge dominant sources of expertise; offer a broad theoretical basis for examining and addressing public problems in health and medicine; and empower patients by distributing sources of expertise. A material rhetorical approach works to respond to these exigencies for RHM by providing a paradigm through which large, intractable controversies involving science and medicine can be addressed. In beginning with an analysis of material exigence, the elements of controversy shaped by the material operations of matter are foregrounded in the analysis. The discourses and discord that organize themselves around and respond to those exigencies can then be informed by understanding the ways in which material shapes arguments and debates, creating opportunities for rhetorically informed responses. Finally, such analysis alerts us to material responses that might offer better ways for modifying exigence and mitigating discord.

EXIGENCIES, RESPONSES, AND SPACES: POSSIBILITIES FOR MODIFYING MATERIAL EXIGENCIES IN VACCINATION CONTROVERSY

Now, with a full discussion and analysis of the material exigencies of vaccine controversy—disease, eradication, injury, and the unknown—what new opportunities for rhetoric could this open up in further study?

To find new discursive responses and spaces, I suggest four primary programs of study that would be critical to operationalizing material exigence into paths for productive change in vaccination controversy and possible intervention for scholars in RHM.

Practitioner-specific study of beliefs and persuasive approaches in clinical contexts. Understanding how vaccines are described and positioned across a health or medical practice could offer key insight into why some practice communities have more positive communication about vaccinations while others experience more tension. Varying forms of pressure, tension, and communication styles about vaccines across a practice would give important insight into the messages that patients receive about vaccines and how those messages might be modified to create more positive communication contexts, both across a practice and in other ones. In the clinic, doctors experience a wide range of constraints, including competing demands on their time, worries about patients with a wide range of needs who might occupy their waiting rooms, and professional expectations and values concerning vaccination. Parents, too, walk into clinical settings with a wide range of competing and conflicting concerns and worries—about side effects, unintended consequences, and irrevocable injuries—that inflect their perspectives on the vaccines that a doctor endorses. Specific, direct methods of working through these issues on an interpersonal level could help lay the groundwork for the mutual understanding that doctors and patients need to have productive, positive conversations about vaccines in these contexts.

Studies of locality and locally directed vaccine beliefs. Understanding the specific articulation of vaccine concerns and support at local levels will help inform what particular concerns groups of parents are responding to. For example, intense, local vaccine *support* might indicate local concern about a sick child or a concentration of illness in a community, which offers key insight into what discourses might be more/less persuasive within a particular context. Such studies have been a hallmark of the work of the Vaccination Research Group (VRG) at Virginia Tech, where we studied and conceptualized the concept of local publics for understanding vaccine decision-making (Lawrence et al.) and studied local outbreaks of pertussis to understand how local incidents of disease shape policy, practice, and public response. This work has indicated that research at the local level is essential for finding the discourses and spaces where a persuasive approach can modify exigence.

Investigating and opening deliberative space. Opening up the spaces where vaccine policies—and health more generally—are discussed to community engagement could work to improve communication about vaccines. Long-term relationship-building with key stakeholders in vaccine-hesitant communities might engage populations of skeptics in health initiatives to ensure continued access to these communities in the case of an outbreak. Bringing people in, soliciting their advice and feedback, and providing services that are responsive to expressed needs will create a space for citizen engagement, with a goal of building long-term public trust to reshape rhetorical situations and begin to modify exigencies. Such measured, incremental goals might not produce robust numbers of vaccinated people or other quantitative outcomes but would instead work slowly and deliberatively toward the exigence changes required to make lasting inroads in hesitant communities. Such an intervention would require researchers in RHM making connections to communities, officials and stakeholders in public health, and possibly local policymakers and legislative bodies.

Global health contexts. Vaccination is obviously not just an American practice, nor is vaccination controversy a uniquely American phenomenon.[4] One additional area that requires additional research is the impact and operation of vaccine discourses worldwide to attain a fuller understanding of the impact that the state, histories of colonialism, and different local responses to disease have on vaccine beliefs. As new diseases such as Zika emerge and the etiology of diseases like Ebola continues to change, international and global health resources will continue to strain and stretch to respond to disease. Vaccination will, no doubt, continue to be an important component of disease response, making it particularly important for mass vaccination campaigns to understand the various international contexts of vaccine acceptance and refusal. RHM scholars will benefit from examining how material exigencies operate across cultures, borders, and governmental and nongovernmental entities.

Across these suggested avenues for future study and intervention is an attention to the finer-grained ways in which local and individual experiences shape the rhetorics of vaccine controversy. Although material exigencies oper-

---

4. The 2017 volume *The Politics of Vaccination: A Global History* outlines some of the major issues related to vaccination and public health worldwide, which are vast and complex.

ate across vaccination, rhetorically informed persuasion maintains that their particular articulations at the local level are likely to be different or at least specific to context and thus must be better understood in order to see what modification of exigence is possible.

Furthermore, the examination of material exigence tells us a lot about strategies that *will not* work at producing more positive communication around vaccinations. Based on the arguments described throughout this text, responses that do one of the following are least attentive to material exigencies and thus unlikely to be persuasive:

- **Arguments that diminish the disease-modifying power of vaccinations.** Such arguments maintain that sanitation or antibiotics or other factors were more impactful than vaccination; such arguments ignore the *purpose for which the vaccine exists—to fight disease.* Denying this primary operation of the object might complicate some elements about the grand narrative of vaccination and its impact on disease, but it will never convince a doctor that vaccination is not a worthwhile practice by undermining its ability to modify disease.
- **Arguments that diminish possibilities of injury that come with vaccinations.** Such arguments, when denied, will likely always be met by shifting, changing counter-concerns that articulate new or confounding concerns about injuries that could result from vaccines. To ignore, dismiss, or even try to disprove such a claim is unlikely to be persuasive since such a stand, too, denies a primary material operation of the object.
- **Totalizing or generalizing arguments that ignore exigencies.** Too often in discussions about vaccinations, dismissal occurs across the spectrum of views on vaccination. Personal experiences of patients are dismissed as misguided worry; risk calculations provided by doctors are dismissed as inapplicable or inaccurate. To dismiss is to ignore exigence; to ignore exigence is to foreclose persuasion, and therefore cannot produce change.

The concept of material exigence demonstrates, rhetorically, why such tactics are ineffective at producing persuasion: they deny opposing exigencies that require modification in situations. However, as some of the examples in this text also show, these are all too often the tactics taken by opponents across the controversy when trying to persuade others—aligning a doctor's advocacy of vaccination with blind trust in science or an uncaring attitude toward the possibilities of illness; associating the concerns of parents with rote assumptions about believing Jenny McCarthy over one's own doctor; assuming that constellations of changing risks are a sign of mistrust or misunderstanding of risk rather than a series of internally consistent mechanisms for dealing with the unknowns of science and medicine. Material exigence, as argued in this book, shows researchers the elements of a situation that *must* be mutually comprehended by rhetors across a situation if persuasion is to be achieved. Denying outright or refusing to comprehend an exigence maintained by another rhetor is not a path to rhetorically informed persuasion.

FUTURE DIRECTIONS FOR RHM RESEARCH IN LARGE CONTROVERSIES INVOLVING SCIENCE AND MEDICINE

Writ large, the concept of material exigence and the material rhetorical approach could continue to be developed to build scholarship in RHM and offer mechanisms for intervention into large, intractable public controversies. In addition to the research and spaces for intervention specific to vaccine controversy discussed above, I suggest a series of additional theories, methods, practices, and sites that might be investigated to improve understanding of the ways in which research, public discourse, and intervention can better inform controversial issues in science and medicine.

Theory—Intercultural Communication

Professional and technical communication research, in particular, has focused on the rhetorical differences required of intercultural communicative efforts. Shaped by the ways that culture affects communication in work environments, intercultural communication research maintains that attending to these differences can help establish the nature of persuasiveness in different contexts, how particular appeals will be received, and which technologies might be accepted by various local cultures. Cultural differences, however, do not just extend to belief systems and ideologies along the boundaries of nation, language, and local or religious customs. Cultures can also encompass ways of thinking or value systems that might inform how exigencies are created and comprehended by various groups, thus affecting what audiences find persuasive in communication. Consequently, intercultural communication paradigms seek to "complicate cultural systems and how interlocutors relate to them," encouraging research and communicative practices that examine not just a person's perspectives on or beliefs about a particular issue but also how the person came to believe those things and hold those opinions (Getto).

This approach, significantly, helps us move toward culture-specific communication practices. Rhetorically informed persuasion opens up possibilities for rhetorical situations to function and for material exigencies to be modified in new and inventive ways, making this a productive theory to adopt in future research.

Theory—Participatory Design and Localization

The principles of participatory design and participatory localization maintain that the end users of any product should be integral throughout all phases of design and development. Similar to user-experience design and usability study, participatory design in professional and technical communication demands that product developers and technical communicators engage with users and audiences to develop materials that respond to their needs, design communication that answers their questions, and overall create situations that solve problems rather than cause them. All these questions, objectives, and practices come together to make outcomes that are user-centered and culturally aware. Participatory localization takes these objectives one step further, demanding that technologies, policies, and practices are redesigned with local users in mind (Agboka, "Decolonial," "Participatory Localization"; Rice and St.Amant), understanding local practices to be different in fundamental ways from the contexts in which products are originally developed.[5]

Participatory design principles evolve out of the practices of the information technology industry, which is constantly vexed with meeting evolving customer needs and creating useful materials for a wide range of users, to include novices and experts alike. Although the concepts may seem far apart, many of the principles of participatory design could inform the most publicly facing communications regarding vaccination—specifically public health communication and policy—as they shape vaccine demands and public response to vaccines.

Some principles of participatory design include seeking stakeholders and partners, not customers; designing *with* not *for*; and eliciting stories about experience (Getto). These principles could drive ways to think about parent participation in development of policies, materials, and information about vaccines. Although bodies like ACIP include "public voices" on their com-

---

5. These principles primarily are deployed in the research cited here in service of social justice efforts as technologies move from the Global North to the Global South; the issue of social justice as it relates to vaccine mandates and vaccine skepticism is an interesting one worth further consideration.

mittees, and legislators express an openness to hearing public concerns on vaccines, the persistence of controversy despite those overtures indicates that these forms of participation are perhaps not as fully formed as they might be. Rather, as participatory design requires, representative users must be included at all stages of product development and deployment, and their concerns must be fully expressed and responded to as they occur.

Methods—Qualitative and Mixed-Methods Research

Qualitative methods—particularly open-ended interviews, mixed-methods studies, ethnographic studies, or methods of digital research and storytelling—would yield the kind of intensive examination of values and beliefs that a rhetorical solution to controversy requires. Although some of these methods have been developed and adopted by some researchers of vaccination (most notably Andrea Kitta's use of folkloric methodologies in *Vaccinations and Public Concern in History*), these tools need to be more widely adopted, used as part of multidisciplinary collaborative research, and incorporated into industry research as well. Furthermore, guided by rhetorical methodologies that examine a wider scope of the landscape, these methods could begin to unpack the complexities of vaccine beliefs as they affect language use. For example, adopting rhetorical situation as a methodology would yield a wider range of information about discussions and beliefs surrounding medicine and science and why they can be so difficult to adjudicate, unearth the exigencies available for modification in various discussions, and examine how these exigencies might be modified.

In the case of vaccination controversy, rhetorical situation as a methodology would guide researchers to interview not just parents who refuse vaccines—as is typical in studies of vaccination controversy—but additional audiences who participate in vaccination practices, such as

> parents who accept vaccination,
> parents who have concerns and skepticisms generally,
> parents who vaccinate according to alternative schedules,
> parents who keep their families "off the grid" in order to avoid vaccines, and
> adults—including seniors and health professionals—who refuse or are skeptical about vaccines for themselves.

Beyond studying just public discourses, however, studying dominant discourses—be they offered by scientists, doctors, or health officials—for their forms of evidence, rhetorical practices, and exigencies is another important component of understanding how situations and rhetoric operate. Expanded qualitative study could give researchers better insight into how parents are persuaded of various vaccine beliefs over time and how those forms of persuasion and arguments inform other beliefs and decisions.

Practices—The Open Stance

Informed by phenomenological, feminist, and community-engaged / action research traditions, this stance maintains that people need to be met where they are, with their viewpoints and worldview accepted and acknowledged as a first practice of research. Instead of seeking persuasion against "wrong thinking" or correction for "misunderstood" science, this stance approaches people curious about and open to the ways that they see the world (Hausman et al.). The open stance is a relationship to research participants that came to be the practice of the VRG at Virginia Tech and key to how that group approaches stakeholders across this issue in order to elicit open responses to and opinions on the issue of vaccination, both those that express support and those that express skepticism.

Approaching people with an open stance has a goal of rhetorically informed persuasion that does not *seek to persuade* but rather *seeks to understand*. This approach not only elicits more open discourse about people's true feelings about vaccination but also offers important insight into how people make the decisions they make and why they hold the values they hold. Although the information gathered from the open stance might be used to inform future attempts at persuasion or other types of intervention, persuasion is not the primary initial goal.

This stance can be adopted by researchers aiming to understand other controversies involving science, medicine, and active public stakeholders. By asking open-ended questions about experiences with illness and medicine, definitions of and parameters for health, and the networks of information that people rely upon for decision-making, researchers can identify the motivations for decision-making as well as alternative spaces for interventions to occur.

The goal of the theories, methods, and practices described above is to open up additional new avenues for understanding material exigencies in large public controversies as a way of adopting a material rhetorical approach to controversies in science and medicine. These theories, methods, and practices are offered as a starting point for rethinking how problems are framed and addressed in the public sphere, moving toward a rhetorical approach to persuasion and away from current stalemates that fail to address the material exigencies of controversies in science and medicine.

CONCLUSION

Vaccination deserves rhetoricity. Vaccines are science turned into medical practice turned into policy, which ultimately makes them historical, cultural, political, public, and individual objects in addition to scientific and medical ones. Therefore, it is imperative that concerns about vaccination and the diseases they prevent are understood as real, valid, and material across the issue, not as simple faulty reasoning, selfishness, pure paternalism, or any of the other quick platitudes that express what vaccination controversy is *really about.*

I have heard various theories about what vaccination is "really about" many times over the years that I have conducted this research, by advocates and skeptics alike. For those eager to share these ideas with me, vaccination controversy is *really* about people not understanding: science, complex risk calculations, the importance of herd immunity, how serious diseases really are, medical paternalism, the commonality of risks, or one of about a dozen already-circulating reasons across the issue. Such theories are not just the idle observations of casual observers. These perspectives form the unstated assumptions of research, are relayed easily in op-ed pieces and online columns, and permeate the discourses of public comments on social media. Embedded in many of these theories is an assumption of deficit, ignorance, and often stupidity on the part of the vaccine skeptic, and control, arrogance, and hubris on the part of the supporter. Such assumptions produce reductive, simple, and usually unhelpful rhetorics, like calling vaccine skeptics "stupid" or "idiots" or insisting on connections between vaccines and conditions that continue to be disproved. Persuasion becomes particularly complicated when one speaker has just called the other ignorant.

I always find it fascinating, though—the same ideas, stated over and over, reflecting the same knee-jerk assumptions about what people know, how they know it, and ultimately, how stupid people *really* are. For actors in the public sphere to reach such a conclusion so easily and so repeatedly despite the fact that such an assumption hasn't led to effective, long-term modes of understanding continues to vex me as a scholar in rhetoric. To return to Aristotle's definition a final time, rhetoric, as the art of seeing the available means of persuasion, is a radical practice of understanding one's audience and of reshaping situations to see where persuasion is possible. As the methods of research and analysis advocated and exercised in this text hopefully show, compelling the public to comply because persuasion has become too difficult is a solution to a problem rooted in a misunderstanding of the rhetorical complexities at play in vaccination. Consequently, considering rhetorically informed persuasive practices must be more widely considered and adopted if reconciliation and improved communication concerning vaccines are to be achieved.

WORKS CITED

"1976 Swine Flu Outbreak Ford Administration Papers." *BACM Research,* 23 Apr. 2013, www.paperlessarchives.com/FreeTitles/1976SWINEFLUOUTBREAK.pdf.

AAP Committee on Practice and Ambulatory Medicine, AAP Committee on Infectious Diseases, AAP Committee on State Government Affairs, AAP Council on School Health, AAP Section on Administration and Practice Management. "Medical versus Nonmedical Immunization Exemptions for Child Care and School Attendance." *Pediatrics,* vol. 138, no. 3, Sept. 2016, article e20162145. doi:10.1542/peds.2016-2145.

Agboka, Godwin Y. "Decolonial Methodologies: Social Justice Perspectives in Intercultural Technical Communication Research." *Journal of Technical Writing and Communication,* vol. 44, no. 3, July 2014, pp. 297–327. *Crossref,* doi:10.2190/TW.44.3.e.

———. "Participatory Localization: A Social Justice Approach to Navigating Unenfranchised/Disenfranchised Cultural Sites." *Technical Communication Quarterly,* vol. 22, no. 1, Jan. 2013, pp. 28–49. *Crossref,* doi:10.1080/10572252.2013.730966.

Ahmed, Syed Sohail, et al. "Antibodies to Influenza Nucleoprotein Cross-React with Human Hypocretin Receptor 2." *Science Translational Medicine,* vol. 7, no. 294, July 2015, pp. 294ra105–294ra105. *stm.sciencemag.org,* doi:10.1126/scitranslmed.aab2354.

Allen, Arthur. *Vaccine: The Controversial Story of Medicine's Greatest Lifesaver.* Norton, 2007.

Andrews, Nick, et al. "Thimerosal Exposure in Infants and Developmental Disorders: A Retrospective Cohort Study in the United Kingdom Does Not Support a Causal Association." *Pediatrics,* vol. 114, no. 3, Sept. 2004, pp. 584–91. *PubMed,* doi:10.1542/peds.2003-1177-L.

Anti-Vaccine Body Count—Home. jennymccarthybodycount.com/. Accessed 3 Sept. 2018.

Arduser, Lora. *Living Chronic: Agency and Expertise in the Rhetoric of Diabetes.* The Ohio State UP, 2017.

Atwell, Jessica E., et al. "Nonmedical Vaccine Exemptions and Pertussis in California, 2010." *Pediatrics,* vol. 132, no. 4, Oct. 2013, pp. 624–30. doi:10.1542/peds.2013-0878.

Barnett, Scot, and Casey Boyle, editors. *Rhetoric, Through Everyday Things.* U Alabama P, 2017.

Barry, John M. *The Great Influenza: The Story of the Deadliest Plague in History.* Penguin Books, 2005.

Baum, Gary. "Hollywood's Vaccine Wars: LA's 'Entitled' Westsiders Behind City's Epidemic." *The Hollywood Reporter,* 10 Sept. 2014, www.hollywoodreporter.com/features/los-angeles-vaccination-rates/.

Bayefsky, Michelle J. "The Ethical Case for Mandating HPV Vaccination." *The Journal of Law, Medicine & Ethics: A Journal of the American Society of Law, Medicine & Ethics,* vol. 46, no. 2, June 2018, pp. 501–10. *PubMed,* doi:10.1177/1073110518782957.

Beck, Ulrich. *Risk Society: Towards a New Modernity.* Translated by Mark Ritter. Sage, 1994.

Bernstein, Susan David. *Confessional Subjects: Revelations of Gender and Power in Victorian Literature and Culture.* U of North Carolina P, 1997.

Bhattacharya, Leena K., et al. "Knowledge and Utilization of Recommended Preventative Vaccines among Young Adults." *Journal of Vaccines & Vaccination,* vol. 4, no. 179, Mar. 2013. *PubMed,* doi:10.4172/2157-7560.1000179

Biesecker, Barbara. "Rethinking Rhetorical Situation from within the Thematic of Différance." *Philosophy and Rhetoric,* vol. 22, no. 2, 1989, pp. 110–30.

Biss, Eula. *On Immunity: An Inoculation.* Graywolf Press, 2015.

Bitzer, Lloyd. "The Rhetorical Situation." *Philosophy and Rhetoric,* vol. 1, no. 1, 1968, pp. 1–11.

Blume, Stuart. "The Erosion of Public Sector Vaccine Production: The Case of the Netherlands." *The Politics of Vaccination: A Global History,* edited by Christine Holmberg, et al., Manchester UP, 2017, pp. 148–73.

Bogost, Ian. *Alien Phenomenology: Or What It's Like to Be a Thing.* U of Minnesota P, 2012.

Bond, Lyndal, and Terry Nolan. "Making Sense of Perceptions of Risk of Diseases and Vaccinations: A Qualitative Study Combining Models of Health Beliefs, Decision-Making and Risk Perception." *BMC Public Health,* vol. 11, no. 943, May 2011. *BioMed Central,* doi:10.1186/1471-2458-11-943.

Bonomo, Melia E., and Michael W. Deem. "Predicting Influenza H3N2 Vaccine Efficacy from Evolution of the Dominant Epitope." *Clinical Infectious Diseases: An Official Publication of the Infectious Diseases Society of America,* vol. 67, no. 7, Apr. 2018. *PubMed,* doi:10.1093/cid/ciy323.

Bowes, Johnathan. "Measles, Misinformation, and Risk: Personal Belief Exemptions and the MMR Vaccine." *Journal of Law and the Biosciences,* vol. 3, no. 3, Nov. 2016, pp. 718–25. *PubMed Central,* doi:10.1093/jlb/lsw057.

Brown, Carolyn. "H1N1 Vaccine and Narcolepsy Link Discovered." *CMAJ : Canadian Medical Association Journal,* vol. 187, no. 12, Sept. 2015, article E371. *PubMed Central,* doi:10.1503/cmaj.109-5118.

Bruni, Frank. "Opinion | The Vaccine Lunacy." *New York Times,* 31 Jan. 2015. *NYTimes.com,* www.nytimes.com/2015/02/01/opinion/sunday/frank-bruni-disneyland-measles-and-madness.html.

"Buck v. Bell." *LII / Legal Information Institute,* www.law.cornell.edu/supremecourt/text/274/200. Accessed 8 Mar. 2019.

Buttenheim, Alison. "Exposure and Vulnerability of California Kindergarteners to Intentionally Unvaccinated Children." *LDI Issue Brief,* vol. 18, no. 1, Oct. 2012, pp. 1–4.

Buttenheim, Alison M., et al. "Conditional Admission, Religious Exemption Type, and Nonmedical Vaccine Exemptions in California before and after a State Policy Change." *Vaccine,* vol. 36, no. 26, 18 June 2018, pp. 3789–93. *PubMed,* doi:10.1016/j.vaccine.2018.05.050.

Campbell, John Angus. "Charles Darwin: Rhetorician of Science." *The Rhetoric of the Human Sciences,* edited by John S. Nelson, Allan Megill, and Donald N. McCloskey, U of Wisconsin P, 1987, pp. 69–86.

Caplan, Arthur. "Ethicist: Why Jim Carrey Is Wrong About Vaccines." *NBC News,* www.nbcnews. com/health/health-news/commentary-why-jim-carrey-wrong-about-vaccines-n385321. Accessed 3 Sept. 2018.

———. "Revoke the License of Any Doctor Who Opposes Vaccination." *Washington Post,* 6 Feb. 2015, www.washingtonpost.com/opinions/revoke-the-license-of-any-doctor-who-opposes -vaccination/2015/02/06/11a05e50-ad7f-11e4-9c91-e9d2f9fde644_story.html?utm_term= .424fad6c5870.

Carey, Matt. "Measles Are Back But Where Is Jenny McCarthy?" *Left Brain Right Brain,* 28 Jan. 2015, leftbrainrightbrain.co.uk/2015/01/28/measles-are-back-but-where-is-jenny-mccarthy/.

Carrion, Melissa L. "'You Need to Do Your Research': Vaccines, Contestable Science, and Maternal Epistemology." *Public Understanding of Science,* vol. 27, no. 3, Apr. 2018, pp. 310–24. *SAGE Journals,* doi:10.1177/0963662517728024.

Carroll, Linda. "Baby's Stroke a Reminder Why the Chickenpox Vaccine Is So Important." *TODAY.com,* 14 Aug. 2018, www.today.com/health/can-chickenpox-cause-stroke-why -vaccine-important-t135593. Accessed 18 Aug. 2018.

Casiday, Rachel Elizabeth. "Children's Health and the Social Theory of Risk: Insights from the British Measles, Mumps, and Rubella (MMR) Controversy." *Social Science and Medicine,* vol. 65, no. 5, Sept. 2007, pp. 1059–70. *Elsevier,* doi.org/10.1016/j.socscimed.2007.04.023. Accessed 14 Mar. 2013.

Ceccarelli, Leah. *Shaping Science with Rhetoric: The Cases of Dobzhansky, Schrodinger, and Wilson.* U of Chicago P, 2001.

Centers for Disease Control and Prevention. "About ACIP." *CDC,* www.cdc.gov/vaccines/acip/ about.html. Accessed 8 May 2013.

———. "Birth-18 Years and Catchup Immunization Schedules for Providers." *CDC,* www.cdc.gov/ vaccines/schedules/hcp/child-adolescent.html. Accessed 26 June 2018.

———. "*Haemophilus Influenzae* | Hib | Clinical Features." *CDC,* www.cdc.gov/hi-disease/ clinicians.html. Accessed 24 Jan. 2019.

———. "Measles | Frequently Asked Questions about Measles in U.S." *CDC,* www.cdc.gov/ measles/about/faqs.html. Accessed 5 Feb. 2018.

———. "Narcolepsy Following Pandemrix Influenza Vaccination in Europe History | Concerns | Vaccine Safety." *CDC,* www.cdc.gov/vaccinesafety/concerns/history/narcolepsy-flu.html. Accessed 18 Aug. 2018.

———. "Past Immunization Schedules." *CDC,* www.cdc.gov/vaccines/schedules/resource-library/ index.html. Accessed 16 Feb. 2018.

———. "Pneumococcal Disease | Surveillance Reporting and Trends." *CDC,* www.cdc.gov/ pneumococcal/surveillance.html. Accessed 24 Aug. 2018.

———. "Rotavirus Vaccine (Rotashield) and Intussusception." *CDC,* www.cdc.gov/vaccines/ vpd-vac/rotavirus/vac-rotashield-historical.htm. Accessed 23 April 2013.

———. "STD Facts—Syphilis (Detailed)." *CDC,* www.cdc.gov/std/syphilis/stdfact-syphilis -detailed.htm. Accessed 11 Jan. 2019.

———. "Vaccines: VPD-VAC/Rotavirus Vaccine (Rotashield ®) and Intussusception." *CDC,* www. cdc.gov/vaccines/vpd-vac/rotavirus/vac-rotashield-historical.htm. Accessed 27 Apr. 2017.

Clary-Lemon, Jennifer. "Archival Research Processes: A Case for Material Methods." *Rhetoric Review,* vol. 33, no. 4, Oct. 2014, pp. 381–402. *Taylor and Francis+NEJM,* doi:10.1080/073501 98.2014.946871.

Colgrove, James. "Immunity for the People: The Challenge of Achieving High Vaccine Coverage in American History." *Public Health Reports,* vol. 122, no. 2, 2007, pp. 248–57. doi:10.1177/003335490712200215.

———. *State of Immunity: The Politics of Vaccination in Twentieth-Century America.* U of California P, 2006.

Collins, Nathan. "Changing Anti-Vaxxers' Minds—Pacific Standard." *Pacific Standard Magazine,* updated 14 June 2017, psmag.com/social-justice/changing-anti-vaccine-minds. Accessed 3 Sept. 2018.

Conis, Elena. "'Do We Really Need Hepatitis B on the Second Day of Life?' Vaccination Mandates and Shifting Representations of Hepatitis B." *Journal of Medical Humanities,* vol. 32, no. 2, June 2011, pp. 155–66. *Crossref,* doi:10.1007/s10912-010-9132-2.

———. *Vaccine Nation: America's Changing Relationship with Immunization.* U of Chicago P, 2016.

Constable, Catherine, et al. "Rising Rates of Vaccine Exemptions: Problems with Current Policy and More Promising Remedies." *Vaccine,* vol. 32, no. 16, Apr. 2014, pp. 1793–97. *PubMed,* doi:10.1016/j.vaccine.2014.01.085.

Coole, Diana H., and Samantha Frost. *New Materialisms: Ontology, Agency, and Politics.* Duke UP, 2013.

Corben, Paul, and Julie Leask. "To Close the Childhood Immunization Gap, We Need a Richer Understanding of Parents' Decision-Making." *Human Vaccines & Immunotherapeutics,* vol. 12, no. 12, 2016, pp. 3168–76. *PubMed,* doi:10.1080/21645515.2016.1221553.

Cortes-Penfield, Nicolas. "Mandatory Influenza Vaccination for Health Care Workers as the New Standard of Care: A Matter of Patient Safety and Nonmaleficent Practice." *American Journal of Public Health,* vol. 104, no. 11, Nov. 2014, pp. 2060–65. *PubMed Central,* doi:10.2105/AJPH.2013.301514.

d'Alessandro, Eugenie, et al. "Determinants of Refusal of A/H1N1 Pandemic Vaccination in a High Risk Population: A Qualitative Approach." *PLoS ONE,* edited by Malcolm Gracie Semple, vol. 7, no. 4, Apr. 2012, e34054. *Crossref,* doi:10.1371/journal.pone.0034054.

Davis, Terry C., et al. "Vaccine Risk/Benefit Communication: Effect of an Educational Package for Public Health Nurses." *Health Education & Behavior,* vol. 33, no. 6, Dec. 2006, pp. 787–801. *Crossref,* doi:10.1177/1090198106288996.

Derrida, Jacques. *Dissemination.* Translated by Barbara Johnson, U of Chicago P, 1983.

Doxtader, Erik. "A Question of Confession's Discovery." *Rhetoric Society Quarterly,* vol. 41, no. 3, May 2011, pp. 267–81. *Crossref,* doi:10.1080/02773945.2011.575329.

Durbach, Nadja. *Bodily Matters: The Anti-Vaccination Movement in England, 1853–1907.* Duke UP, 2005.

Edbauer, Jenny. "Unframing Models of Public Distribution: From Rhetorical Situation to Rhetorical Ecologies." *Rhetoric Society Quarterly,* vol. 35, no. 4, Sept. 2005, pp. 5–24.

Einstein Shorr, Rebecca. "If Jenny McCarthy Were Jewish, She'd Have to Vaccinate." *Tablet Magazine,* 13 Feb. 2015, www.tabletmag.com/jewish-life-and-religion/188861/jewish-vaccine-obligation.

Fahnestock, Jeanne. "Accommodating Science: The Rhetorical Life of Scientific Facts." *Written Communication,* vol. 15, no. 3, July 1998, pp. 330–50.

———. "Rhetoric of Science: Enriching the Discipline." *Technical Communication Quarterly,* vol. 14, no. 3, July 2005, pp. 277–86.

———. *Rhetorical Figures in Science.* Oxford UP, 2003.

Feikin, D. R., et al. "Individual and Community Risks of Measles and Pertussis Associated with Personal Exemptions to Immunization." *JAMA*, vol. 284, no. 24, Dec. 2000, pp. 3145–50.

Fine, Paul, et al. "'Herd Immunity': A Rough Guide." *Clinical Infectious Diseases*, vol. 52, no. 7, Apr. 2011, pp. 911–16. *Oxford Academic*, doi:10.1093/cid/cir007.

Flake, Emily. "Daily Cartoon: Monday, February 2nd." *NewYorker.com*, Feb. 2015, www. newyorker.com/cartoons/daily-cartoon/daily-cartoon-monday-february-2nd-measles -disneyland.

Flannery, Brendan. "Interim Estimates of 2017–18 Seasonal Influenza Vaccine Effectiveness— United States, February 2018." *Morbidity and Mortality Weekly Report (MMWR)*, vol. 67, 2018. *www.cdc.gov*, doi:10.15585/mmwr.mm6706a2.

Gargano, Lisa M., et al. "Seasonal and 2009 H1N1 Influenza Vaccine Uptake, Predictors of Vaccination, and Self-Reported Barriers to Vaccination among Secondary School Teachers and Staff." *Human Vaccines*, vol. 7, no. 1, Jan. 2011, pp. 89–95. *Crossref*, doi:10.4161/hv.7.1.13460.

Gastañaduy, Paul A., et al. "A Measles Outbreak in an Underimmunized Amish Community in Ohio." *New England Journal of Medicine*, vol. 375, no. 14, Oct. 2016, pp. 1343–54. *Taylor and Francis+NEJM*, doi:10.1056/NEJMoa1602295.

Getto, Guiseppe. "Designing for Engagement: Intercultural Communication and/as Participatory Design." *Rhetoric, Professional Communication and Globalization*, vol. 5, no. 1, 2014, pp. 44–66, www.rpcg.org/index.php?journal=rpcg&page=article&op=view&path%5B%5D=76. Accessed 15 June 2017.

Gold, Jenny. "Measles Outbreak Sparks Bid to Strengthen Calif. Vaccine Law." *NPR.org*, www.npr. org/sections/health-shots/2015/02/05/383988632/vaccination-exemption-blamed-for -measles-spread-in-california. Accessed 1 Sept. 2018.

Gouge, Catherine. "'No Single Path': Desire Lines and Divergent Pathographies in Health and Medicine." *Methodologies for the Rhetoric of Health and Medicine*, edited by Lisa Melonçon and J. Blake Scott, Routledge, 2018, pp. 115–37.

Gouge, Catherine, and John Jones. "Wearables, Wearing, and the Rhetorics That Attend to Them." *Rhetoric Society Quarterly*, vol. 46, no. 3, May 2016, pp. 199–206. doi:10.1080/027739 45.2016.1171689.

Graham, S. Scott. *The Politics of Pain Medicine: A Rhetorical-Ontological Inquiry*. U of Chicago P, 2015.

Graham, S. Scott, and Carl Herndl. "Multiple Ontologies in Pain Management: Toward a Postplural Rhetoric of Science." *Technical Communication Quarterly*, vol. 22, no. 2, Apr. 2013, pp. 103–25. *Taylor and Francis+NEJM*, doi:10.1080/10572252.2013.733674.

Grant, Lenny, Amy Reed, and Heidi Y. Lawrence. "Medicolegal Rhetorics: Medicine as Arbitrator in Competing Discourses about Disease and Disability." Rhetoric Society of America Conference, 29 May 2016, Atlanta, GA. Conference Panel.

Grant, Lenny, et al. "Vaccination Persuasion Online: A Qualitative Study of Two Provaccine and Two Vaccine-Skeptical Websites." *Journal of Medical Internet Research*, vol. 17, no. 5, May 2015, article e133. *EBSCOHost*, doi:10.2196/jmir.4153.

Gross, Alan G., et al. "Argument and 17th-Century Science: A Rhetorical Analysis with Sociological Implications." *Rhetoric and the Early Royal Society*, edited by Tina Skouen and Ryan Stark. Brill, 2014, pp. 128–57.

Gullion, Jessica Smartt, et al. "Deciding to Opt Out of Childhood Vaccination Mandates." *Public Health Nursing*, vol. 25, no. 5, Oct. 2008, pp. 401–08. *PubMed*, doi:10.1111/j.1525-1446.2008. 00724.x.

Haas, Angela. "Wired Wombs: A Rhetorical Analysis of Online Infertility Support Communities." *Webbing Cyberfeminist Practice: Communities, Pedagogies, and Social Action,* edited by Kristine Blair, et al., Hampton, 2009, pp. 61–84.

Habakus, Louise Kuo, and Mary Holland. *Vaccine Epidemic: How Corporate Greed, Biased Science, and Coercive Government Threaten Our Human Rights, Our Health, and Our Children.* Skyhorse, 2011.

Haglin, Kathryn. "The Limitations of the Backfire Effect." *Research & Politics,* vol. 4, no. 3, July 2017, pp. 1–5. *Crossref,* doi:10.1177/2053168017716547.

Hall, Kimberly. "Selfies and Self-Writing: Cue Card Confessions as Social Media Technologies of the Self." *Television & New Media,* vol. 17, no. 3, Mar. 2016, pp. 228–42. *Crossref,* doi:10.1177/1527476415591221.

Happe, Kelly E. *The Material Gene: Gender, Race, and Heredity after the Human Genome Project.* New York UP, 2016.

Haraway, Donna Jeanne. *Simians, Cyborgs, and Women: The Reinvention of Nature.* Routledge, 1990.

Harding, Sandra G. *The Science Question in Feminism.* Cornell UP, 1993.

Harlan, John Marshall. *HENNING JACOBSON, v. COMMONWEALTH OF MASSACHUSETTS.* www.law.cornell.edu/supremecourt/text/197/11. Accessed 3 Sept. 2018.

Harman, Graham. *Tool-Being: Heidegger and the Metaphysics of Objects.* Open Court, 2011.

Hausman, Bernice L. *Anti/Vax: Reframing the Vaccination Controversy.* Cornell UP, 2019.

———. "Immunity, Modernity, and the Biopolitics of Vaccination Resistance." *Configurations,* vol. 25, no. 3, June 2017, pp. 279–300. doi:10.1353/con.2017.0020.

———. *Mother's Milk: Breastfeeding Controversies in American Culture.* Routledge, 2003.

———. *Viral Mothers: Breastfeeding in the Age of HIV/AIDS.* U of Michigan P, 2010.

Hausman, Bernice L., Mecal Ghebremichael, Phillip Hayek, and Erin Mack. "'Poisonous, Filthy, Loathsome, Damnable Stuff': The Rhetorical Ecology of Vaccination Concern." *The Yale Journal of Biology and Medicine,* vol. 87, no. 4, Dec. 2014, pp. 403–16.

Hausman, Bernice L., Heidi Lawrence, Susan West Marmagas, Lauren Fortenberry, and Clare Dannenberg. "H1N1 Vaccination and Health Beliefs in a Rural Community in the Southeastern United States: Lessons Learned." *Critical Public Health.* Available online 20 Dec. 2018. doi:10.1080/09581596.2018.1546825. Accessed 14 Jan. 2019.

Healy, C. Mary, and Larry K. Pickering. "How to Communicate with Vaccine-Hesitant Parents." *Pediatrics,* vol. 127, no. 1, 2011, pp. S127–33. *American Academy of Pediatrics.* Accessed 19 Mar. 2012. *PubMed,* doi:10.1542/peds.2010-1722S.

Healy, Jack, and Michael Paulson. "Vaccine Critics Turn Defensive over Measles." *New York Times,* 30 Jan. 2015, www.nytimes.com/2015/01/31/us/vaccine-critics-turn-defensive-over-measles.html.

Hendrix, Kristin S., et al. "Ethics and Childhood Vaccination Policy in the United States." *American Journal of Public Health,* vol. 106, no. 2, Feb. 2016, pp. 273–78. *PubMed,* doi:10.2105/AJPH.2015.302952.

Hennessy, Kathleen. "How a Bout of Rotavirus Made Me Appreciate Vaccines." *Narrative Inquiry in Bioethics,* vol. 6, no. 3, 2016, pp. 161–63. *Project MUSE,* doi:10.1353/nib.2016.0073.

Hillson, Christina M., et al. "Adult Vaccination." *Primary Care: Clinics in Office Practice,* vol. 38, no. 4, Dec. 2011, pp. 611–32. *Crossref,* doi:10.1016/j.pop.2011.07.003.

Hiltzik, Michael. "Jenny McCarthy: Anti-Vaxxer, Public Menace." *LATimes.com*, www.latimes. com/business/hiltzik/la-fi-mh-jenny-mccarthy-antivaxxer-public-menace-20150127-column. html. Accessed 2 Aug. 2018.

Hobson-West, Pru. "Understanding Vaccination Resistance: Moving Beyond Risk." *Health, Risk, & Society*, vol. 5, no. 3, 2003, pp. 273–83. doi:10.1080/13698570310001606978.

Holmberg, Christine, et al. *The Politics of Vaccination: A Global History.* Manchester UP, 2017.

Hunsaker, David M., and Craig Smith. "The Nature of Issues: A Constructive Approach to Situational Rhetoric." *Western Speech Communication*, vol. 40, no. 3, 1976, pp. 144–56.

"International Memorial for Vaccine Victims—NVIC." *National Vaccine Information Center (NVIC)*, www.nvic.org/Vaccine-Memorial.aspx. Accessed 8 Sept. 2018.

Israeli, Eitan, et al. "Guillain–Barré Syndrome—A Classical Autoimmune Disease Triggered by Infection or Vaccination." *Clinical Reviews in Allergy & Immunology*, vol. 42, no. 2, Apr. 2012, pp. 121–30. *Springer Link*, doi:10.1007/s12016-010-8213-3.

Jack, Jordynn. "Leviathan and the Breast Pump: Toward an Embodied Rhetoric of Wearable Technology." *Rhetoric Society Quarterly*, vol. 46, no. 3, May 2016, pp. 207–21. doi:10.1080/ 02773945.2016.1171691.

Jenner, Edward. *An Inquiry into the Causes and Effects of the Variolae Vaccinae, A Disease Discovered in Some of the Western Counties of England, Particularly Gloucestershire, and Known by the Name of the Cow Pox.* 2009. *Project Gutenberg*, www.gutenberg.org/ebooks/29414?msg= welcome_stranger.

Jacobson, Robert M., et al. "A Taxonomy of Reasoning Flaws in the Anti-Vaccine Movement." *Vaccine*, vol. 25, no. 16 Apr. 2007, pp. 3146–52. *Crossref,* doi:10.1016/j.vaccine.2007.01.046.

Johnson, Jenell. *American Lobotomy.* U of Michigan P, 2014.

———. "'A Man's Mouth Is His Castle': The Midcentury Fluoridation Controversy and the Visceral Public." *Quarterly Journal of Speech*, vol. 102, no. 1, Jan. 2016, pp. 1–20. *Crossref,* doi:10. 1080/00335630.2015.1135506.

Kaler, Amy. "Health Interventions and the Persistence of Rumour: The Circulation of Sterility Stories in African Public Health Campaigns." *Social Science & Medicine*, vol. 68, no. 9, May 2009, pp. 1711–19. *Crossref,* doi:10.1016/j.socscimed.2009.01.038.

Kata, Anna. "Anti-Vaccine Activists, Web 2.0, and the Postmodern Paradigm—An Overview of Tactics and Tropes Used Online by the Anti-Vaccination Movement." *Vaccine*, vol. 30, no. 25, May 2012, pp. 3778–89. *Crossref,* doi:10.1016/j.vaccine.2011.11.112.

———. "A Postmodern Pandora's Box: Anti-Vaccination Misinformation on the Internet." *Vaccine*, vol. 28, no. 7, Feb. 2010, pp. 1709–16. *Crossref,* doi:10.1016/j.vaccine.2009.12.022.

Keränen, Lisa. *Scientific Characters: Rhetoric, Politics, and Trust in Breast Cancer Research.* U of Alabama P, 2010.

Kessler, Molly Margaret. "Wearing an Ostomy Pouch and Becoming an Ostomate: A Kairological Approach to Wearability." *Rhetoric Society Quarterly*, vol. 46, no. 3, May 2016, pp. 236–50. doi:10.1080/02773945.2016.1171693.

Khazan, Olga. "LA's Richest Neighborhoods Have Vaccination Rates Lower Than the Poorest Parts of Africa." *The Atlantic*, 16 Sept. 2014, www.theatlantic.com/health/archive/2014/09/ wealthy-la-schools-vaccination-rates-are-as-low-as-south-sudans/380252/.

Kitta, Andrea. *Vaccinations and Public Concern in History: Legend, Rumor, and Risk Perception.* Routledge, 2012.

Kloeblen, A. S., and S. S. Batish. "Understanding the Intention to Permanently Follow a High Folate Diet among a Sample of Low-Income Pregnant Women According to the Health Belief Model." *Health Education Research,* vol. 14, no. 3, June 1999, pp. 327–38.

Koerber, Amy. *Breast or Bottle? Contemporary Controversies in Infant-Feeding Policy and Practice.* U of South Carolina P, 2013.

———. *From Hysteria to Hormones: A Rhetorical History.* Pennsylvania State UP, 2018.

Kolodziejski, Lauren R. "Harms of Hedging in Scientific Discourse: Andrew Wakefield and the Origins of the Autism Vaccine Controversy." *Technical Communication Quarterly,* vol. 23, no. 3, July 2014, pp. 165–83. doi:10.1080/10572252.2013.816487.

Kukla, Rebecca. *Mass Hysteria: Medicine, Culture, and Mothers' Bodies.* Rowman & Littlefield, 2011.

Largent, Mark A. *Vaccine: The Debate in Modern America.* Johns Hopkins UP, 2012.

Latour, Bruno, and Steve Woolgar. *Laboratory Life: The Construction of Scientific Facts.* Princeton UP, 2013.

Lawrence, Heidi Y. "Fear of the Irreparable: Narratives in Vaccination Rhetoric." *Narrative Inquiry in Bioethics,* vol. 6, no. 3, 2016, pp. 205–09. *Crossref,* doi:10.1353/nib.2016.0060.

———. "Healthy Bodies, Toxic Medicines: College Students and the Rhetorics of Flu Vaccination." *Yale Journal of Biology and Medicine,* vol. 87, no. 4, Dec. 2014, pp. 423–37.

———. "Medicolegal Rhetorics and Vaccination Policy and Practice." *Rhetoric Society of America Conference,* May 29, 2016, Atlanta, GA. Conference Paper Presentation.

———. "When Patients Question Vaccines: Considering Vaccine Communication through a Material Rhetorical Approach." *Rhetoric of Health & Medicine,* vol. 1, no. 1–2, May 2018, pp. 161–78. *Crossref,* doi:10.5744/rhm.2018.1010.

Lawrence, Heidi Y., Bernice L. Hausman, and Clare Dannenberg. "Reframing Medicine's Publics: The Local as a Public of Vaccine Refusal." *Journal of Medical Humanities,* vol. 35, no. 2, June 2014, pp. 111–29. *Crossref,* doi:10.1007/s10912-014-9278-4.

Leask, Julie, et al. "Communicating with Parents about Vaccination: A Framework for Health Professionals." *BMC Pediatrics,* vol. 12, no. 1, Dec. 2012, article 154. *Crossref,* doi:10.1186/1471-2431-12-154.

Lehmkuhl, Markus, and Hans Peter Peters. "Constructing (Un-)Certainty: An Exploration of Journalistic Decision-Making in the Reporting of Neuroscience." *Public Understanding of Science,* vol. 25, no. 8, Nov. 2016, pp. 909–26. *SAGE Journals,* doi:10.1177/0963662516646047.

Lerner, Adam S. "Medical Narratives in Rhetorical Context: Ethically Researching Anti-Vaccinationists." *Technical Communication Quarterly,* vol. 27, no. 1, Jan. 2018, pp. 80–92. *Crossref,* doi:10.1080/10572252.2018.1399750.

"LIS > Bill Tracking > HB1342 > 2016 Session." *LIS: Virginia's Legislative Information Center.* lis.virginia.gov/cgi-bin/legp604.exe?161+sum+HB1342. Accessed 3 Sept. 2018.

Loe Fisher, Barbara. "The Moral Right to Conscientious, Philosophical and Personal Belief Exemption to Vaccination." *National Vaccine Information Center (NVIC),* www.nvic.org/informed-consent.aspx. Accessed 3 Sept. 2018.

Looper, Philip, et al. "Student and Faculty Perceptions about Mandatory Influenza Vaccinations on a Health Sciences Campus." *Journal of American College Health,* vol. 65, no. 7, Oct. 2017, pp. 513–17. *PubMed,* doi:10.1080/07448481.2017.1341899.

Lundgren, Britta, and Martin Holmberg. "Pandemic Flus and Vaccination Policies in Sweden." *The Politics of Vaccination: A Global History,* edited by Christine Holmberg, et al., Manchester UP, 2017, pp. 260–87.

Majumder, Maimuna S., et al. "Substandard Vaccination Compliance and the 2015 Measles Outbreak." *JAMA Pediatrics,* vol. 169, no. 5, May 2015, pp. 494–95. *PubMed,* doi:10.1001/jamapediatrics.2015.0384.

Malatino, Hilary. "Biohacking Gender: Cyborgs, Coloniality, and the Pharmacopornographic Era." *Angelaki,* vol. 22, no. 2, Apr. 2017, pp. 179–90. doi:10.1080/0969725X.2017.1322836.

Malkowski, Jennifer. "Confessions of a Pharmaceutical Company: Voice, Narrative, and Gendered Dialectics in the Case of Gardasil." *Health Communication,* vol. 29, no. 1, Jan. 2014, pp. 81–92. doi:10.1080/10410236.2012.719178.

Marmagas, Susan, et al. *Cumberland Plateau Health District 2009–2010 Flu Season Vaccine Study Final Report,* 31 Aug. 2011, www.vaccination.english.vt.edu/wp-content/uploads/2015/04/Vaccine_Report_Final_CPHD-2.pdf. Government Report.

MatoAna5. *Ana's Montage- Vaccine Induced Autism.* YouTube, www.youtube.com/watch?v=NMh5EaeLFMU. Accessed 18 Aug. 2018.

Mayo Clinic. "Infectious Diseases—Symptoms and Causes." https://www.mayoclinic.org/diseases-conditions/infectious-diseases/symptoms-causes/syc-20351173. Accessed 8 Mar. 2019.

McGee, Michael C., and John R. Lyne. "What Are Nice Folks Like You Doing in a Place Like This?" *The Rhetoric of the Human Sciences,* edited by John Nelson, et al., U of Wisconsin P, 1987, pp. 381–406.

Melançon, Lisa K. "Bringing the Body Back through Performative Phenomenology." *Methodologies for the Rhetoric of Health and Medicine,* edited by Lisa Melançon and J. Blake Scott, Routledge, 2018, pp. 96–114.

Melançon, Lisa, and J. Blake Scott. "Manifesting a Scholarly Dwelling Place in *RHM.*" *Rhetoric of Health and Medicine,* vol. 1, no. 1–2, Winter/Spring 2018, pp. i–x. doi:10.5744/rhm.2018.1001.

———, editors. *Methodologies for the Rhetoric of Health and Medicine.* Routledge, 2018.

Miller, Carolyn. "Genre as Social Action." *Quarterly Journal of Speech.* vol. 70, 1984, pp. 151–67.

Miller, Elaine R., et al. "Deaths Following Vaccination: What Does the Evidence Show?" *Vaccine,* vol. 33, no. 29, June 2015, pp. 3288–92. *PubMed Central,* doi:10.1016/j.vaccine.2015.05.023.

Miller, Mark, et al. "Control and Eradication." *Disease Control Priorities in Developing Countries,* edited by Dean T. Jamison, et al., 2nd ed., World Bank, 2006, chapter 62. *PubMed,* www.ncbi.nlm.nih.gov/books/NBK11763/.

Mol, Annemarie. *The Body Multiple: Ontology in Medical Practice.* Duke UP, 2002.

Mol, Annemarie, and John Law. "Embodied Action, Enacted Bodies: The Example of Hypoglycemia." *Body and Society,* vol. 10, no. 2–4, 2004, pp. 43–62.

Molyneux, David H., et al. "Disease Eradication, Elimination and Control: The Need for Accurate and Consistent Usage." *Trends in Parasitology,* vol. 20, no. 8, Aug. 2004, pp. 347–51. *PubMed,* doi:10.1016/j.pt.2004.06.004.

Mooney, Chris. "Study: You Can't Change an Anti-Vaxxer's Mind." *Mother Jones,* 3 Mar. 2014, www.motherjones.com/environment/2014/03/vaccine-denial-psychology-backfire-effect/. Accessed 3 Sept. 2018.

National Vaccine Information Center (NVIC). "About National Vaccine Information Center." www.nvic.org/about.aspx. Accessed 8 Mar. 2019.

Navin, Mark. *Values and Vaccine Refusal: Hard Questions in Ethics, Epistemology, and Health Care.* Routledge, 2017.

Nelson, John S., et al., editors. *The Rhetoric of the Human Sciences: Language and Argument in Scholarship and Public Affairs.* U of Wisconsin P, 1987.

New, Suzanne J., and Martyn L. Senior. "'I Don't Believe in Needles': Qualitative Aspects of a Study into the Uptake of Infant Immunisation in Two English Health Authorities." *Social Science & Medicine*, vol. 33, no. 4, Jan. 1991, pp. 509–18. *Crossref*, doi:10.1016/0277-9536 (91)90333-8.

Nitsch-Osuch, Aneta, and Lidia Bernadeta Brydak. "Influenza Vaccinations of Health Care Personnel" [Article in Polish]. *Medycyna Pracy*, vol. 64, no. 1, 2013, pp. 119–29.

Nossal, G. J. V. "Vaccines of the Future." *Vaccine*, vol. 29, no. 4, Dec. 2011, pp. D111–15. *PubMed*, doi:10.1016/j.vaccine.2011.06.089.

Nyhan, Brendan. "Vaccine Opponents Can Be Immune to Education." *New York Times*, 8 May 2014, www.nytimes.com/2014/05/09/upshot/vaccine-opponents-can-be-immune-to-education.html.

Nyhan, Brendan, and Jason Reifler. "Does Correcting Myths about the Flu Vaccine Work? An Experimental Evaluation of the Effects of Corrective Information." *Vaccine*, vol. 33, no. 3, Jan. 2015, pp. 459–64. *PubMed*, doi:10.1016/j.vaccine.2014.11.017.

Nyhan, Brendan, et al. "Effective Messages in Vaccine Promotion: A Randomized Trial." *Pediatrics*, Apr. 2014, pp. e835–e842. *AAP News and Journals Gateway*, doi:10.1542/peds.2013-2365.

"Of Vaccines and Vacuous Starlets." *The Economist*, Jan. 2015, www.economist.com/united-states/2015/01/29/of-vaccines-and-vacuous-starlets.

Offit, Paul. *The Cutter Incident: How America's First Polio Vaccine Led to the Growing Vaccine Crisis*. Yale UP, 2005.

———. *Deadly Choices: How the Anti-Vaccine Movement Threatens Us All*. Basic Books, 2010.

Offit, Paul A., and Charles J. Hackett. "Addressing Parents' Concerns: Do Vaccines Cause Allergic or Autoimmune Diseases?" *Pediatrics*, vol. 111, no. 3, Mar. 2003, pp. 653–59. *AAP News & Journals Gateway*, doi:10.1542/peds.111.3.653.

Omer, Saad B., et al. "Vaccine Refusal, Mandatory Immunization, and the Risks of Vaccine-Preventable Diseases." *The New England Journal of Medicine*, vol. 360, no. 19, May 2009, pp. 1981–88. *PubMed*, doi:10.1056/NEJMsa0806477.

Opel, Douglas J., et al. "Development of a Survey to Identify Vaccine-Hesitant Parents: The Parent Attitudes about Childhood Vaccines Survey." *Human Vaccines*, vol. 7, no. 4, Apr. 2011, pp. 419–25. *Crossref*, doi:10.4161/hv.7.4.14120.

Oshinsky, David M. *Polio: An American Story*. Oxford UP, 2006.

Oster, Emily, and Geoffrey Kocks. "After a Debacle, How California Became a Role Model on Measles." *New York Times*, 20 Jan. 2018, www.nytimes.com/2018/01/16/upshot/measles-vaccination-california-students.html.

Parker, Sarah K., et al. "Thimerosal-Containing Vaccines and Autistic Spectrum Disorder: A Critical Review of Published Original Data." *Pediatrics*, vol. 114, no. 3, Sept. 2004, pp. 793–804. *PubMed*, doi:10.1542/peds.2004-0434.

Pender, Kelly. *Being at Genetic Risk: Toward a Rhetoric of Care*. Pennsylvania State UP, 2018.

———. "Genetic Subjectivity in Situ: A Rhetorical Reading of Genetic Determinism and Genetic Opportunity in the Biosocial Community of FORCE." *Rhetoric and Public Affairs*, vol. 15, no. 2, 2012, pp. 319–50.

Perelman, Chaim, and Lucie Olbrechts-Tyteca. *The New Rhetoric: A Treatise on Argument*. Translated by John Wilkinson and Purcell Weaver. U of Notre Dame P, 1991.

Poland, Gregory A. "MMR Vaccine and Autism: Vaccine Nihilism and Postmodern Science." *Mayo Clinic Proceedings*, vol. 86, no. 9, Sept. 2011, pp. 869–71. *Crossref*, doi:10.4065/mcp.2011.0467.

Prematunge, Chatura, et al. "Factors Influencing Pandemic Influenza Vaccination of Healthcare Workers—A Systematic Review." *Vaccine*, vol. 30, no. 32, July 2012, pp. 4733–43. *PubMed*, doi:10.1016/j.vaccine.2012.05.018.

Price, Cristofer, et al. "Prenatal and Infant Exposure to Thimerosal from Vaccines and Immunoglobulins and Risk of Autism." *Pediatrics*, vol. 126, no. 4, Oct. 2010, pp. 656–64. *AAP News & Journals Gateway*, pediatrics.aappublications.org/content/early/2010/09/13/peds.2010-0309. Accessed 19 Aug. 2018.

Principi, Nicola, and Susanna Esposito. "Vaccine-Preventable Diseases, Vaccines and Guillain-Barré Syndrome." *Vaccine*, June 2018. *PubMed*, doi:10.1016/j.vaccine.2018.05.119.

Reavis, Rachael D., et al. "A Self-Affirmation Exercise Does Not Improve Intentions to Vaccinate among Parents with Negative Vaccine Attitudes (and May Decrease Intentions to Vaccinate)." *PLoS ONE*, vol. 12, no. 7, July 2017, article e0181368. *PLoS Journals*, doi:10.1371/journal.pone.0181368.

Reed, Amy R. "Building on Bibliography: Toward Useful Categorization of Research in Rhetorics of Health and Medicine." *Journal of Technical Writing and Communication*, vol. 48, no. 2, Apr. 2018, pp. 175–98. *SAGE Journals*, doi:10.1177/0047281616667904.

Retzbach, Andrea, and Michaela Maier. "Communicating Scientific Uncertainty: Media Effects on Public Engagement with Science." *Communication Research*, vol. 42, no. 3, Apr. 2015, pp. 429–56. *SAGE Journals*, doi:10.1177/0093650214534967.

Rice, Jenny. *Distant Publics: Development Rhetoric and the Subject of Crisis*. U of Pittsburgh P, 2012.

Rice, Rich, and Kirk St.Amant. *Thinking Globally, Composing Locally Rethinking Online Writing in the Age of the Global Internet*. Utah State UP, 2018.

Rosenstock, Irwin. "Historical Origins of the Health Belief Model." *Health Education Monographs* 2.4 (1974): 328–35.

———. "Why People Use Health Services." *The Milbank Memorial Fund Quarterly*, vol. 44, no. 3, July 1966, pp. 94–127. *Crossref*, doi:10.2307/3348967.

Salmon, Daniel. A., et al. "Health Consequences of Religious and Philosophical Exemptions from Immunization Laws: Individual and Societal Risk of Measles." *JAMA*, vol. 282, no. 1, July 1999, pp. 47–53.

Salmon, Daniel A., et al. "Public Health and the Politics of School Immunization Requirements." *American Journal of Public Health*, vol. 95, no. 5, May 2005, pp. 778–83. *Crossref*, doi:10.2105/AJPH.2004.046193.

Sanevax. "Theresa from Massachusettes." *Sanevax.org*, sanevax.org/theresa-from-massachusettes/. Accessed 14 Jan. 2019.

Schlussel, Debbie. "Bimbo Science: 'Doctor' Jenny McCarthy & the New McCarthyism." *Debbie Schlussel*, www.debbieschlussel.com/3052/bimbo-science-doctor-jenny-mccarthy-the-new-mccarthyism/. Accessed 3 Sept. 2018.

Schuster, Mary L., et al. "Medico-Legal Collaboration Regarding the Sex Offender: Othering and Resistance." *Rhetoric of Health & Medicine*, vol. 1, no. 1–2, May 2018, pp. 90–131. doi:10.5744/rhm.2018.0005.

Schwartz, Jason L., and Arthur L. Caplan. "Vaccination Refusal: Ethics, Individual Rights, and the Common Good." *Primary Care: Clinics in Office Practice*, vol. 38, no. 4, Dec. 2011, pp. 717–28. *Crossref*, doi:10.1016/j.pop.2011.07.009.

Schwartzman, Roy, et al. "Rhetoric and Risk." *Poroi*, vol. 7, no. 1, Feb. 2011, article 9. *Crossref*, doi:10.13008/2151-2957.1087.

Scott, J. Blake. *Risky Rhetoric: AIDS and the Cultural Practices of HIV Testing.* Southern Illinois UP, 2014.

Scott, Jennifer L., et al. "Rhetoric, Ebola, and Vaccination: A Conversation among Scholars." *Poroi,* vol. 11, no. 2, Dec. 2015, pp. 1–26. doi:10.13008/2151-2957.1232.

Seely, Hart. *Pieces of Intelligence: The Existential Poetry of Donald Rumsfeld.* Free Press, 2009.

Segal, Judy Z. *Health and the Rhetoric of Medicine.* Southern Illinois UP, 2008.

Shaw, Jana, et al. "Immunization Mandates, Vaccination Coverage, and Exemption Rates in the United States." *Open Forum Infectious Diseases,* vol. 5, no. 6, June 2018, article ofy130. *PubMed,* doi:10.1093/ofid/ofy130.

Sisson, Paul. "Measles Outbreak Fuels Exemption Debate." *Sandiegouniontribune.com,* www.sandiegouniontribune.com/news/health/sdut-measles-disneyland-outbreak-vaccination-exemptions-2015jan17-htmlstory.html. Accessed 1 Sept. 2018.

Smith, Craig R., and Scott Lybarger. "Bitzer's Model Reconstructed." *Communication Quarterly,* vol. 44, no. 2, Mar. 1996, pp. 197–213. *Crossref,* doi:10.1080/01463379609370010.

Stewart, Ashley. "I Will Always Ask You If Your Child Is Vaccinated, and Here's Why." www.scarymommy.com/is-your-child-vaccinated/. Accessed 2 Sept. 2018.

"Sweden: WHO and UNICEF Estimates of Immunization Coverage." *Unicef.org.* United Nations Children's Fund (UNICEF), 5 July 2016, data.unicef.org/wp-content/uploads/country _profiles/Sweden/Immunization_swe.pdf. Accessed 8 Sept. 2017.

Taylor, Marisa. "Disneyland Measles Outbreak Sheds Light on Anti-Vaccine Movement." *Al Jazeera America,* 23 Jan. 2015, america.aljazeera.com/articles/2015/1/23/measles-disneyland -anti-vaccine.html.

Tell, David. "Beyond Mnemotechnics: Confession and Memory in Augustine." *Philosophy and Rhetoric,* vol. 39, no. 3, 2006, pp. 233–53. *Crossref,* doi:10.1353/par.2006.0026.

Teston, Christa. *Bodies in Flux: Scientific Methods for Negotiating Medical Uncertainty.* U of Chicago P, 2017.

———. "Rhetoric, Precarity, and mHealth Technologies." *Rhetoric Society Quarterly,* vol. 46, no. 3, May 2016, pp. 251–68. doi:10.1080/02773945.2016.1171694.

TheAmateurScientist. *The Jenny McCarthy Song. YouTube,* www.youtube.com/watch?v=0v_85tAey9s. Accessed 3 Sept. 2018.

US Food and Drug Administration (FDA). "Thimerosal in Vaccines." *FDA.gov,* 3 Mar. 2010, www.fda.gov/BiologicsBloodVaccines/SafetyAvailability/VaccineSafety/UCM096228. Accessed 9 Nov. 2011.

"Vaccination Rates in Elite Los Angeles Schools Now Worse Than in Southern Sudan." *IFLScience.* www.iflscience.com/health-and-medicine/vaccination-rates-plummet-elite-los-angeles -schools/. Accessed 1 Sept. 2018.

Vaccines.gov. "Vaccine Ingredients." US Department of Health and Human Services. www.vaccines.gov/basics/vaccine_ingredients/index.html. Accessed 3 Sept. 2018.

Vatz, Richard. "The Myth of the Rhetorical Situation." *Philosophy and Rhetoric,* vol. 6, no. 3, 1973, pp. 154–61.

"Viola Davis, Common, Richard Madden, Liv Warfield." *Live with Jimmy Kimmel,* season 13, episode 31, ABC, Abc.go.com. Accessed 26 Feb. 2015.

Virginia Department of Health (VDH). "School Requirements." 20 Mar. 2013, http://www.vdh.virginia.gov/immunization/requirements/. Accessed 23 Apr. 2013.

Vogel, Gretchen. "Why a Pandemic Flu Shot Caused Narcolepsy." *Science | AAAS,* 1 July 2015, www.sciencemag.org/news/2015/07/why-pandemic-flu-shot-caused-narcolepsy.

Wakefield, Andrew, et al. "Ileal-Lymphoid-Nodular Hyperplasia, Non-Specific Colitis, and Pervasive Developmental Disorder in Children." *The Lancet,* vol. 351, no. 9103, Feb. 1998, pp. 637–41. *Web EBSCOHost.* Accessed 31 Oct. 2011.

Walker, Kenny C. "Rhetorical Properties of Scientific Uncertainties: Public Engagement in the Carson Scholars Program." *Poroi,* vol. 10, no. 1, Jan. 2014. *Crossref,* doi:10.13008/2151-2957. 1178.

Walker, Kenny, and Lynda Walsh. "'No One Yet Knows What the Ultimate Consequences May Be': How Rachel Carson Transformed Scientific Uncertainty Into a Site for Public Participation in Silent Spring." *Journal of Business and Technical Communication,* vol. 26, no. 1, Jan. 2012, pp. 3–34. *SAGE Journals,* doi:10.1177/1050651911421122.

Walloch, Karen L. *The Antivaccine Heresy: Jacobson v. Massachusetts and the Troubled History of Compulsory Vaccination in the United States.* U of Rochester P, 2015.

Wang, Eileen, et al. "Nonmedical Exemptions from School Immunization Requirements: A Systematic Review." *American Journal of Public Health,* vol. 104, no. 11, Nov. 2014, pp. e62–84. *PubMed,* doi:10.2105/AJPH.2014.302190.

Willrich, Michael. *Pox: An American History.* Penguin, 2011.

World Health Organization. "South Sudan: WHO and UNICEF Estimates of Immunization Coverage: 2017." *WHO,* www.who.int/immunization/monitoring_surveillance/data/ssd.pdf. Accessed 13 Jan. 2019.

———. "WHO | Statement on Narcolepsy and Vaccination." *WHO,* www.who.int/vaccine_safety/ committee/topics/influenza/pandemic/h1n1_safety_assessing/narcolepsy_statement/en/. Accessed 4 Aug. 2018.

Wong, Li Ping, and I-Ching Sam. "Ethnically Diverse Female University Students' Knowledge and Attitudes toward Human Papillomavirus (HPV), HPV Vaccination and Cervical Cancer." *European Journal of Obstetric Gynecology and Reproductive Biology,* vol. 148, no. 1, 2010, pp. 90–95. doi:10.1016/j.ejogrb.2009.10.002.

Wyatt, H. V. "The Popularity of Injections in the Third World: Origins and Consequences for Poliomyelitis." *Social Science and Medicine,* vol. 19, no. 9, 1984, pp. 911–15.

Yang, Z. Janet. "Too Scared or Too Capable? Why Do College Students Stay Away from the H1N1 Vaccine?" *Risk Analysis,* vol. 32, no. 10, 2012, pp. 1703–16. doi:10.1111/j.1539-6924.2012.01799.x.

Zibners, Lara. "Ask before They Play to Keep Chickenpox, Pertussis and Measles Away." *Shot of Prevention,* 15 July 2014, shotofprevention.com/2014/07/15/ask-before-they-play-to-keep -chickenpox-pertussis-and-measles-away/.

INDEX

Made in the USA
Middletown, DE
02 September 2020

9 781606 495940